PRACTICING ORAL HISTORY TO CONNECT UNIVERSITY TO COMMUNITY

Practicing Oral History to Connect University to Community illustrates best practices for using oral histories to foster a closer relationship between institutions of higher learning and the communities in which they are located.

Using case studies, the book describes how to plan and execute an oral history project that can help break down walls and bring together universities and their surrounding communities. It offers advice on how to locate funding sources, disseminate information about the results of a project, ensure the long-term preservation of the oral histories collected and incorporate oral history into the classroom. Bringing together "town and gown," the book demonstrates how different communities can work together to discover new research opportunities and methods for preserving history.

Supported by examples, sample forms and online resources, the book is an important resource both for oral historians and those working to improve relationships between university institutions and their neighboring communities.

Beverly B. Allen received her M.A. in History from the University of Missouri, St. Louis and her M.S. in Library Science from the University of Illinois, Urbana/ Champaign. She is currently University Archivist at Colorado State University, Pueblo and has written several articles about building ethnically diverse archival collections, including "Yo Soy Colorado: Three Collaborative Hispanic Cultural Heritage Initiatives" (*Collaborative Librarianship*, 2012).

Fawn-Amber Montoya received her Ph.D. from the University of Arizona in 2007. Montoya currently serves as the Director of the Honors Program at Colorado State University, Pueblo, and edited the collection *Making an American Workforce: The Rockefellers and the Legacy of Ludlow* (2014).

Practicing Oral History

Series editor, Nancy MacKay

Museums, historical societies, libraries, classrooms, cultural centers, refugee organizations, elder care centers, and neighborhood groups are among the organizations that use oral history both to document their own communities and to foster social change. The *Practicing Oral History* series addresses the needs of these professionals with concise, instructive books about applying oral history best practices within the context of their professional goals.

Titles fall into one of three areas of applied oral history. The first format addresses a specific stage or skill within the oral history process. The second addresses the needs of professional communities who use oral history in their field. The third approach addresses the way oral history can be used to make an impact. Each title provides practical tools, ethical guidelines and best practices for conducting, preserving, and using oral histories within the framework of acknowledged standards and best practices.

Readers across a wide array of disciplines will find the books useful, including education, public history, local history, family history, communication and media, cultural studies, gerontology, documentary studies, museum & heritage studies, and migration studies.

Recent titles in the series:

Practicing Oral History with Immigrant Narrators
Carol McKirdy

Story Bridges
A Guide for Conducting Intergenerational Oral History Programs
Angela Zusman

Practicing Oral History to Improve Public Policies and Programs
Marella Hoffman

Practicing Critical Oral History
Connecting School and Community
Christine K. Lemley

Practicing Oral History to Connect University to Community
Beverly B. Allen and Fawn-Amber Montoya

For more information, or to place orders visit Routledge, Practicing Oral History, www.routledge.com/Practicing-Oral-History/book-series/POHLCP

PRACTICING ORAL HISTORY TO CONNECT UNIVERSITY TO COMMUNITY

Beverly B. Allen and
Fawn-Amber Montoya

With José Antonio Ortega

Routledge
Taylor & Francis Group

NEW YORK AND LONDON

First published 2019
by Routledge
711 Third Avenue, New York, NY 10017

and by Routledge
2 Park Square, Milton Park, Abingdon, Oxon, OX14 4RN

Routledge is an imprint of the Taylor & Francis Group, an informa business

Library of Congress Cataloging-in-Publication Data
A catalog record for this title has been requested

ISBN: 978-1-138-60547-3 (hbk)
ISBN: 978-1-138-60548-0 (pbk)
ISBN: 978-0-429-46807-0 (ebk)

Typeset in Bembo and Stone Sans
by Florence Production Ltd, Stoodleigh, Devon, UK

DEDICATION

The authors dedicate this book to all those who have donated their valuable collections to the Colorado State University-Pueblo Archives so that the history of the Colorado Chicano/a Movement can continue to be preserved and made available to future generations of students, faculty and the general public.

CONTENTS

FIGURES AND TABLES

Figures

Tables

ABOUT THE AUTHORS

Beverly B. Allen, M.A. History, University of Missouri, St. Louis; M.S. Library Science, University of Illinois, Urbana/Champaign. University Archivist/ Professor, Colorado State University, Pueblo; formerly Reference Archivist, Emory University; Archivist, Missouri Historical Society; independent archives consultant. Member, Society of American Archivists; Society of Rocky Mountain Archivists.

Fawn-Amber Montoya, Ph.D. History, University of Arizona; M.A. History, University of Arizona; B.A. History Brigham Young University. Colorado State University, Pueblo, Professor of History, Director of Honors. Member, Western History Association; National Association of Chicano/Chicana Studies.

José Antonio Ortega, B.A., History, Chicano/a Studies minor, Colorado State University, Pueblo. Exhibits and Collection Coordinator, El Pueblo History Museum; formerly Archives Assistant, Colorado State University, Pueblo; Library Assistant, Pueblo Public Library District.

FOREWORD

Some years ago, I was given the task of forming an oral history program. The college where I worked as a librarian wanted a way to improve relations with the surrounding inner-city community and oral history seemed like the perfect vehicle for community engagement, so I enthusiastically jumped right in. My professional training and experience is in academic librarianship and, though I had taken an oral history workshop and conducted some interviews, I hadn't a clue what it meant to set up and operate an oral history program. I didn't know how to sell the community on the idea, or how to create an atmosphere where students and the community engage to increase understanding. Here are some more things I needed to know but didn't: how to track the many steps in conducting an oral history, and for that matter, how to keep records *about everything;* how to set up protocols for transcribing, processing, and preserving interviews; how to nudge faculty to integrate oral history into class projects; how to reach out to the community; and most ironically, how best to spend the generous budget that came with the grant-funded program.

After a year or so of networking, attending conferences, and experimenting, we ended up with an oral history program that I am proud of. Our accomplishments include a few undergraduate courses, community training workshops, public events, and more than 70 oral histories now available through the college and local public libraries. Along the way, I learned that university/community oral history is a valued model for pedagogy and community engagement. I met librarians and faculty members in institutions around the country who, like me, were working in isolation to build their oral history program; basically reinventing the wheel.

Oh, how I wish I had had the book that you hold in your hands today. In *Practicing Oral History to Connect University to Community*, archivist Beverly Allen and professor Fawn-Amber Montoya have answered the questions I and my colleagues had, provided a roadmap for negotiating the murky waters that connect community and academia, and addressed questions that I hadn't thought to ask or that have arisen in the digital world that is our new reality.

Though the community/university relationship is often presented as a *town vs gown* dichotomy, it is rarely that simple. Within the academic setting there are usually two players in an oral history program, the library or archives whose goal is to build oral history collections for future research, and the faculty whose goal is to give students a quality learning experience. Add to this mix the community members whose goal is to have a voice in history, and a triangular dance arises around these three focus points: preservation and access, pedagogy, and making history. As Allen and Montoya point out, the most successful oral history programs embrace this tension to find a balance and benefit from the three-way collaboration. The book greatly benefits from the distinct voices of the archivist (Allen) and the faculty member (Montoya).

The authors use their own institution, Colorado State University-Pueblo, and four additional academic/community oral history programs as case studies. Their community of Pueblo, Colorado, with a population of more than 100,000, is a hub city in southern Colorado with a strong Hispanic population (more than 50 percent, according to census statistics), which includes both old Hispanic families and recent immigrants. About 18 percent of the city population holds a bachelor's degree or higher. In contrast, only 25 percent of the CSU-Pueblo student body identifies as Hispanic and less than half come from the immediate area. The authors use this demographic divide between university and community as a focal point for the challenges of engaging with the community.

Each of the other four case studies from around the United States—the Oregon Multicultural Archives at Oregon State University in Corvallis; the Archives and Special Collections Department of Northeastern University Libraries in Boston, Massachusetts; the Samuel Proctor Center for Oral History at the University of Florida, Gainesville; and the Special Collections Department of Texas A&M University in Commerce, Texas—sponsor oral history programs which tell the unique story of their own communities through oral history, and give students a learning experience of a lifetime.

I'm sure you will agree with the authors that "a strong, long-term relationship between the university and the community is always win–win. Such relationships take time, patience, persistence, and compromise, and it is always worth the effort. Oral history, also known as the people's history, is a great step towards cultivating these long-term relationships."

Enjoy the book!

Nancy MacKay
Berkeley, California
April 2017

PREFACE

This book is designed for the "gown:" faculty, students, and archivists working in an academic setting. These groups in particular will find it useful:

- Alumni associations interested in preserving the stories of their alumni.
- Archivists interested in beginning a new oral history project or complementing an existing one.
- Educators who use oral histories to supplement their classroom materials and to connect their students with family members and to the historical past.
- University administrators and faculty to illustrate best practices and examples of how to bridge the social, economic, and educational divides that can exist with the community.

Despite the different perspectives of community members, community institutions, educators and the university, we expect readers can learn:

- How to build bridges between community and institutions of higher education.
- How to create positive community outreach activities.
- What resources are necessary to begin the process of oral history collection.
- How to collect and preserve a community's history.
- How to make collections accessible.

Organization

The chapters will be organized in the following manner: community relationships, community outreach, funding, process, ethics and best practices, publicizing, classroom experiences, preservation, and community collaborations. We will use case studies from universities around the United States to illustrate oral history best practices applied in real life. These case studies will illustrate innovative and collaborative approaches to oral history collection and ways to bridge the town and gown divide. Besides using examples from our institution, Colorado State University-Pueblo, we have included case study examples from the Samuel Proctor Oral History Program at the University of Florida, Northeastern University (Boston), Oral History Program at the University of Florida, Archives and Special Collections, Oregon Multicultural Archives at Oregon State University, and the Texas War and Memory Project at East Texas A&M-Commerce.

The Appendices include samples of print or online versions of promotional materials, oral history release forms, sample interview questions, biographical sheets, and a list of additional web and print based resources.

Who We Are

The main authors of the book are CSU-Pueblo university faculty: University Archivist Beverly B. Allen, and Dr. Fawn-Amber Montoya, history professor and Director of Honors Program.

Beverly B. Allen—"I've been an archivist for over 30 years, working primarily at universities and historical societies. I did my first oral history project way back in the 1970s, when I worked at the Missouri Historical Society, and we were celebrating the 75th anniversary of the St. Louis World's Fair of 1904. We thought it would be 'fun' to try and find some folks who had actually attended the Fair and interview them. We had no idea what we were getting into and I think we probably made every mistake in the book.

When I came to CSU-Pueblo to continue building the newly established ethnic history and diversity collection, I found oral history to be a particularly useful tool in working with existing communities, and especially for gathering ethnic history. Some societies have more of an oral tradition than a written one, so if you're unwilling to do oral history, you may find the culture that much harder to document."

Fawn-Amber Montoya—"My family has lived in southern Colorado since the mid-1800s. I live about five miles from where my father grew up. Pueblo has always been a place that I have seen as home. A number of years ago, I came across an oral interview that my great grandfather recorded in the 1970s with the Colorado Historical Society. I loved being able to hear his voice, and to also be able to use his interview for research was a rewarding and heartfelt experience. I would love for my community to be able to record their stories, but I would also love for my students to be able to use these interviews as sources for historical research. Interviewing individuals for class assignments has allowed students a glimpse into their past and the opportunity to rethink how they view their community. The collection of oral histories we've built at CSU-Pueblo has also helped me to better connect with the community. I have met people who were active in the Chicano/a Movement. I know them from their activism today, but the oral interviews have helped me to learn more about where they got their start."

One chapter is written by CSU-Pueblo graduate **José Ortega**. He majored in history and minored in Chicano/a Studies, and belongs to the Phi Alpha Theta national history honor society. Ortega has worked for the CSU-Pueblo University Archives for more than three years, primarily on the Colorado Chicano/a Movement Archives. He has organized and processed the United Mexican American Students collection and conducted interviews with Chicano/a activists. Mr. Ortega is from the community of Pueblo and has many family members who are community activists; who have donated their documents and oral histories to the CSU-Pueblo Archives. Ortega works at El Pueblo History Museum where he is Exhibits and Collections Coordinator.

Note on Terms: Latino/a and Chicano/a

Throughout the text we will use the terms Latino/a and Chicano/a to address individuals and communities that either identify as Chicano/a or Latino/a. Latino/a is how the US census identifies people of Latin American descent. Chicano/a is a group within Latino/a that is of Mexican-American descent that acknowledges their unique history as a Mestizo (mixed blood) people. Chicanos have deep roots in the southwestern United States and many of their ancestors lived in the southwest before it was Mexico and Spain. They embrace their native heritage and identity as a colonized and oppressed people and use this to frame their worldview.

ACKNOWLEDGMENTS

The authors would like to thank the following people for their assistance, without which this book could not have been written: Juan Federico "Freddie Freak" Miguel Arguello Trujillo, José Esteban Ortega, Rita J. Martinez and the rest of the Colorado Chicano/a Movement Archives Advocates for their support and promotion of the Archives; our case study participants, Natalia Fernandez, Paul Ortiz, Andrea Weddle, and Joan Krizack, who graciously agreed to be interviewed and provide examples of their practices for this book; Rhonda Gonzales, Dean of the Library at CSU-Pueblo, for her advocacy and enthusiasm, funding, and support for Allen's sabbatical; William Folkestad, Dean of the College of Humanities and Social Sciences at CSU-Pueblo, for approving Montoya's sabbatical; Provost Rick Kremenski, and President Lesley DiMare for funding to build and continue our oral history program; the David and Lucille Packard Foundation, the Statewide Internet Authority (Colorado), and the Colorado Association of Libraries International Library Cultural Exchange Interest Group for additional funding to build and preserve the Colorado Chicano/a Movement Archives; our wonderful and dedicated students, José Antonio Ortega, Paul Valdez, and Isabel Soto-Luna, who spent many hours transcribing oral histories; our outside reviewers and colleagues Ashley Martinez and Cyn Nelson, who read the draft of the book, and provided valuable feedback; Leigh Grinstead who shared her expertise on digital preservation; CSU, Pueblo President Timothy P. Mottet for his support and encouragement; and last, but far from least, the Pueblo community which responded so positively and generously to our documentation efforts.

Beverly B. Allen
Fawn-Amber Montoya

INTRODUCTION

Practicing Oral History to Connect University to Community addresses how colleges or universities can connect with and reflect the rich histories of the communities nearby, or who have large archival holdings relating to these communities. We will give examples from throughout the United States of how institutions are actively collecting oral histories within their neighboring communities, and also collaborating with oral history projects that originated within the community. These institutions are models for how university faculty and staff can interact with community members and organizations despite disparities in age, educational level, and length of time in the community. The examples illustrate how the community and the university can collaborate to preserve and celebrate their rich history and how archival collections contribute to the preservation of this history. We also feel that these institutions illustrate the kinds of oral history projects currently being completed and the ways universities are working with communities across the United States.

This publication addresses a divide that sometimes occurs between communities and institutions of higher education located near their respective communities. There has been an historical and social perception that universities and colleges are detached from the daily lives of members of their communities. Historically there has been a desire from universities to separate themselves from the communities either to protect themselves or to study in "splendid isolation". With the creation of a "campus model" with living spaces, food, and recreation and student life all on campus, it eliminated the need for community spaces for university students further emphasizing this divide.[1]

This separation has created a common perception that the university is an "ivory tower" in which faculty develop and engage with ideas and philosophies that appear to be unreasonable or impractical, and that real world experiences separate the ideals of the university from the everyday experiences of its neighboring communities.

Members of neighboring communities, or the "town," might perceive the university as disconnected and impractical. Town residents may feel that the university community takes advantage of local resources, housing, shopping, and schools without returning anything. This perception may feel like an unequal and unfair relationship and many times the university may appear to be unconcerned. Because of the size of the university and the money spent on buildings there may be misconceptions from the community about the income of employees at the university, their workload, and how much discretionary money is available for new projects.

Tom Heaney, in his article, "The Illusive Ground Between Town and Gown," addresses the division that may occur between the town and the gown with division potentially creating feelings of hostility or animosity between these two physical spaces or among the employees of the university and the local residents. The relationships between town and gown may have been strained in the past if university agendas conflicted with or diverged from the interests of the community. There may be attempts to align the mission of the university or college through Service Learning which may have students learning to be connected with community organizations and needs.[2]

The American Association of State Colleges and Universities has encouraged universities to establish relationships with the community in which they are "engaged institutions" and "regional stewards." "The most desirable town-gown relationship type—the harmonious relationship—reflects the blending of high effort and high comfort levels."[3] The main reason for this encouragement is based on experiences when there are negative relationships between town and gown. These issues can relate to land development concerns and negative and destructive behavior of students in the community.[4]

Oral history can serve as a way to bridge this town and gown divide. By creating a partnership or collaboration the community can come to learn more about the reality of university resources and the types of scholarship being produced. The university can see first-hand how it has impacted the community over time. This type of work creates spaces for community/university dialogue, can expand the university's strategic plan, and show the community that the university is committed to investing in the area where they are located.

What do we mean by 'community' or 'town'? Communities may also, of course, be defined by geography, a common history or common social, economic, political or professional interest. For example, a community could consist of a group of medical workers (occupation), Asian-Americans (ethnic origins), working class people (economic status), or Sikhs (religion). Community is defined very broadly in this book.

The important point is that divides can exist between the university and the neighboring communities based on a variety of factors. These could be real divides that the university and the community may acknowledge or they may be perceived only by one group.

What is oral history and why is it important? According to the Oral History Association, "oral history is a field of study and a method of gathering, preserving and interpreting the voices and memories of people, communities, and participants in past events."[5] Oral histories can be audio- or video-recorded interviews, which may be transcribed, indexed or summarized, and placed in a library or archives for long-term preservation and access by researchers.

Oral history is a useful tool to capture the stories of both ordinary and extraordinary individuals; these personal stories help fill out the historical record. For example, a book about the Civil Rights Movement presents a picture of the facts and sequence of events, but when personal stories and recollections are added, such as the experience of a Freedom Rider describing exactly what he experienced in a southern prison, then it engages the reader/listener. History, as is often taught in secondary schools, can strike students as dull and boring, but when eyewitness accounts are added, the past comes to life and they experience the human connection from one generation to another.

Don Ritchie, in his book *Doing Oral History*, referenced the work of Charles L. Sullivan in his book, *Gathering at the River: South Mississippi's Camp Meetings*, in which Sullivan explains the relevance of an oral history project. "That is the reason for doing oral history: to ask the questions that have not been asked and to collect the reminiscences that otherwise would be lost."[6]

Oral histories can also give a voice to those who have been underrepresented in traditional historical accounts. For example, ethnic groups, LGBTQ communities, and working class individuals will have a different perspective from that presented in mainstream narratives. At CSU-Pueblo, for example, our interviews with Chicano/a activists provide a valuable and vastly different perspective on current events than newspaper accounts of the 1960s and 1970s.

Are oral interviews really any different from personal letters which recount the writer's experience of historical events at a point in time? If these documents are considered valid for historical inquiry, then why not oral histories?

Though it can be difficult sometimes to assess the accuracy of oral history narratives, just as with other primary sources, at times it may be the only way to capture the history of a certain group, time, and place.[7] In many cases, the information may exist nowhere else—stories, anecdotes, traditions, and songs bring a human dimension to the dry bones of history. Oral histories can provide the backstory to photographs, documents, and other primary sources. Moreover, oral histories should stand equally with other primary and secondary sources for historians to critically evaluate in their research. Oral histories allow us to have a glimpse into the past and come to better understand how history has shaped the experience of the individual, permits us to see what daily life was like and how memory has impacted our collective history.

Valerie Raleigh Yow, in her book, *Recording Oral History: A Practical Guide for Social Scientists*, addresses how oral histories are qualitative research allowing the researcher to go more in depth. Yow explores the idea that researchers can use oral histories to frame a history that makes sense and that these interviews will be used in the context of other sources. These interviews may not just be limited to historians but could be used by anthropologists and sociologists among other disciplines.[8]

Furthermore, many cultures have a stronger oral tradition than a written one or have an oral tradition in addition to a written one. Conducting oral histories may be the only way to document that history. Both Native American and African cultures have very strong and venerable oral traditions. Are these traditions to be ignored solely because they are oral?

In the foreword to Patricia Preciado Martin's book, *Songs My Mother Sang to Me*, historian Vicki Ruiz writes that the relevance of oral histories of Mexican-American women is that "one sees their history through their eyes."[9] She argues that Mexican women's participation in the economy and in the community has been overlooked by historians and that the oral histories in the text demonstrate the relevance of women's work as essential to the community.[10]

About Our Case Studies

Colorado State University-Pueblo, located in Pueblo, Colorado, is a regional comprehensive university—a university that grants bachelors, masters and doctoral degrees. It is located 100 miles south of Denver, and 100 miles from the Colorado/New Mexico border. Pueblo, Colorado has a strong industrial base and has been acknowledged as a labor community with the local steel mill at the turn of the 19th century bringing an ethnically diverse workforce to the region. The community of Pueblo is the industrial and economic hub of southeastern Colorado. The communities surrounding it, specifically to the south, were linked to the steel mill through the coal mining industry because the coal was mined in order to heat the materials that made the steel. The areas to the east are linked to Pueblo through the Arkansas River Valley. This has created a region that has made Pueblo the political, economic, and social hub of the region.[11]

CSU-Pueblo sits at the edge of the city limits at the top of a hill. This location, the ethnic diversity of the community (at least 25 percent of CSU-Pueblo's student population is Latino/a compared to the city of Pueblo where over 50 percent of its population identify as Latino/a) and the economic resources of the university have given CSU-Pueblo a reputation to many in the community as being uninvolved in the community and of not representing its Latino/a population. To further illustrate the town/gown disparity, only 18 percent of Pueblo's population has a bachelor's degree or higher and the median family income was approximately $35,000. Less than half of CSU-Pueblo's student population comes from the region.

In order to bridge some of this divide, the CSU-Pueblo's University Archives and Special Collections has made it part of its mission to collect, preserve, and make accessible materials that document southern Colorado's ethnic heritage and diversity. Pueblo, Colorado has a number of archives, including the Steel-works Center of the West, and the Pueblo City County Library, but until 2009, there was no active collecting of oral histories that focused on ethnic heritage and diversity. In addition, the Chicano/a Studies program at CSU-Pueblo had very little material to be able to teach students about the history of Chicano/a's in the area. In order to expand the collections, the archivist, Jay Trask, wrote a grant that assisted in this new desire to collect local histories. In the past CSU-Pueblo's archival collection has been more focused on the history of the institution, but in the past 10 years, faculty and staff have actively worked to expand the archival collections at the university to more closely reflect the rich ethnic diversity of southeastern Colorado. Much of this was made possible with a grant from the David and Lucille Packard Foundation in 2008. The University Archives has actively collected personal documents, audiovisual materials and alternative publications from community members and also began an oral history project that includes the stories of local residents who were active during the Civil Rights movement of the 1960s, as well as current activism relating to Columbus Day protests.[12] The Archives has also documented the experiences of Latino/a veterans in the Korean, Vietnam and more recent Gulf wars. This collection has come to be called the Southeastern Colorado Ethnic Heritage and Diversity Archives (SCEHADA).[13]

The Archives' community oral history project has expanded the university's relationship with the community, so that now community organizations are beginning to turn to the university to collaborate on community focused oral history projects. The oral history project was initiated during the initial process of collecting papers related to the Chicano/a Movement. What we found was that while there was a wealth of material in papers and manuscripts, there were many activists in our community. These activists had been active in the movement and shared their experiences with people with whom they had participated in the movement, but this information was neither transferred into the collective memory of the community nor into official histories at the state or national level.

Today, Oregon State University (OSU) has more than 28,000 students with over 20 percent of the population from a diverse ethnic background. About 61 percent of the student population is from Oregon. The 2014 graduating class consisted of 3,000+ students with as few as 300 from the surrounding community.[14] According to 2016 census data, over 55,000 people lived in Corvallis, the city closest to Oregon State, with 7.4 percent being Latino/a, and around 1 percent African-American. 56 percent of the population has a bachelor's degree or higher. 82 percent of Oregon's population is White, 12 percent is Latino/a, 4 percent Asian and 2 percent African-American.[15] While the majority of the state does not have a lot of ethnic diversity, the Oregon Multicultural Archives was established in 2005 as an initiative of the Oregon State University Libraries to document the history and contributions of numerous ethnic communities in Oregon, including African-American, Asian-American, Latino/a and Native Americans. The Oregon Multicultural Archives has been in existence for longer than CSU-Pueblo's Ethnic Heritage and Diversity Archives and their collection is broader because of the size and resources of the institution.

According to Natalia Fernandez, Oregon Multicultural Librarian, an initiative that has worked particularly well for them has been increasing access to collections by digitizing documents and posting them online.[16] Their oral history collection centers on the diverse voices of the campus community through interviews with faculty, staff, and alumni. In addition, Fernandez has participated in a project recording the stories of a migrant farm worker community in Oregon. This project is a collaboration with *Juntos*—a program at the college that helps parents of high school students keep their children in school and encourages access to college.[17] Fernandez has given presentations about developing relationships between tribal communities and non-tribal cultural heritage institutions with examples from the Oregon Multicultural Archives given at the 2013 Association of Tribal Archives. Fernandez has spoken and written extensively about OSU's collaborative projects. These presentations and publications highlight how oral histories have become central to telling the stories of ethnically diverse populations in the United States. These projects illustrate how to work with the community to achieve positive results.[18]

The Archives and Special Collections Department of Northeastern University Libraries (Boston) has had similar experiences to both CSU-Pueblo and Oregon State. Northeastern University is an urban university, located in the Fenway, Roxbury and Back Bay neighborhoods of Boston, Massachusetts, which has a population of 656,000. According to 2017 census data, Boston is 47 percent White, 24.4 percent African-American, 8.9 percent Asian, 3.9 percent two or more races, and 17.5 percent Latino/a.[19] Northeastern University, on the other hand, has a student body with about the same number of Whites (56 percent), but with a greater disparity in relation to other ethnic groups (7 percent Latino/a, 13 percent Asian), and especially African-Americans (5 percent).[20] Boston's median income is $53,900, and 43.9 percent of the population holds a bachelor's degree.[21] The disparity between the number of African-Americans enrolled at the university and their representation in the city of Boston created pressure for the university to better coexist with the African-American community of Roxbury. This allowed the Archives and Special Collections department to create a project that focused on the documentation of Roxbury.

Like CSU-Pueblo, Northeastern initially began collecting ethnic materials with grant funding. In 1998, an initial project funded by the National Historical Publications and Records Commission (NHPRC) began. Today, Northeastern continues to collect, preserve and make available historical records that were at risk of being destroyed of Boston's African-American, Chinese, gay and lesbian, and Latino/a communities. Also, like CSU-Pueblo, Northeastern uses oral history to help connect with neighboring ethnic communities in Boston. For example, a collection of oral histories relating to Boston's Lower Roxbury African-American community has recently been opened for research.[22]

Giordana Mecagni, Head of Archives and Special Collections, says that Northeastern is currently working on a project, "Our Marathon: The Boston bombing digital archive," which is a crowd-sourced archives of pictures, videos, stories, and social media.[23] Crowd sourcing allows for participants in multiple locations to share their stories and materials. This also enables the collection to be shaped by the community. The project was initiated by the residents of Boston with assistance from faculty and students from the English department and the library's Digital Scholarship group. As part of the project, the team conducted oral histories with first responders, police and victims of the bombing.[24]

Although Northeastern still has many challenges relating to its community, it has found oral history to be a valuable tool both for the university and the community to foster understanding by telling another side of Boston's history as well as to diversify the archival record. It has also empowered the community to tell its own story, and visibly demonstrated that their narratives have significance beyond themselves, thus engendering pride and ownership of the historical record. Indeed, Northeastern's experience with oral history has encouraged them to expand the program, and a professional recording studio has recently been established in the library, in part to help facilitate the interview process. Also, like CSU-Pueblo, Northeastern has found collecting oral histories a way to expose students to primary sources, and to connect them in a very tangible way to living history. Likewise, the community has benefited from sharing and preserving their individual and collective memories.[25]

The Samuel Proctor Oral History Program (SPOHP) is a stand-alone oral history center in the College of Liberal Arts and Sciences at the University of Florida. The university is situated in the city of Gainesville, Florida, with a population of 128,640. Gainesville's population is 64.9 percent White, 23 percent African-American, 6.9 percent Asian, 2.9 percent two or more races, and 10 percent Latino/a.[26] The University of Florida is made up of somewhat fewer Whites (55.76 percent), and a higher percentage of Latino/as (21 percent) and Asians (8 percent), about the same number of mixed race (3.1 percent), but a much smaller percentage of African-Americans (6.2 percent).[27] Gainesville's median income is $34,290 and 43.2 percent of residents hold a bachelor's degree.[28] Founded in 1967, the Proctor Center has conducted more than 6,500 interviews which are then turned over to the University Archives to preserve and make accessible. Every year, the program trains students, researchers, interns, and volunteers in the techniques of oral history and they gather, preserve, and promote living histories of individuals from all walks of life. They engage in research projects across the country and host public programs as well. SPOHP currently has five ongoing major projects: the Alachua County African-American History Project (AAHP), Mississippi Freedom Project (MFP), Veterans History Project (VHP), the Latina/o Diaspora in the Americas Project (LDAP), and the Native American History Project (NAHP). These projects illustrate the diversity that is possible within an oral history program.[29]

The East Texas War and Memory Project is an oral and public history project instituted by the Special Collections Department of Texas A&M University at Commerce (Texas A&M Commerce). Texas A&M Commerce is located about 60 miles northeast of Dallas. The city of Commerce has around 8,000 residents with the university adding around another 11,000 to the overall population. About 54 percent of Commerce is White with about 11 percent being Latino/a and over 20 percent identifying as African-American. 30 percent of the community has a bachelor's degree or higher.[30] About 51 percent of the campus is of Anglo-American descent with non-Anglo students coming from a variety of backgrounds including 21 percent from African-American descent and around 16 percent being Latino/a. The university is similar to the demographic makeup of the community around it.[31] The project collects and preserves the stories of military veterans and immediate family members in order to create a public and collective memory for current generations without any connections to twentieth century conflicts. Texas A&M Commerce, like CSU-Pueblo, has made extensive use of undergraduate students to conduct oral history interviews.[32]

Joint Stewardship

Collaboration, while not exactly a new concept for universities, may rub against the culture of an institution. Collaboration requires academics to give up some control over things. This may include how the project is conducted and sometimes even control over the oral histories. So, universities may not automatically look to their communities to gather oral histories, preferring more traditional methods of documentation, such as paper collections.

But collaboration with the local community can utilize the strengths of both town and gown to yield many benefits to both university and community. The community receives professional assistance to document its history, and the university is able to collect materials it might not otherwise be able to. Furthermore, collaboration can provide valuable experiential education for students involved in collecting oral histories, as well as research opportunities that they would have to otherwise travel for. Experiential education allows students to have hands on experiences that connect them to the subject matter in their courses.[33] Oral history is an example of experiential education because students are involved in the collection of stories related to history and they are creating primary resources that, when deposited into a library or archives, enters the historical record for widespread use over time. It affords the university a priceless opportunity to connect with its community in a meaningful way, and to make community members aware that the university and its archives are not just a central place for the creation and preservation of knowledge but also to envision the archivist as a steward of historical materials.

Joint stewardship requires an attitude adjustment among academics. University partners can start by learning and employing the principles of Joel Wurl's approach, which he writes about in his pioneering article, "Ethnicity as Provenance: In Search of Values and Principles for Documenting the Immigrant Experience." Wurl urges the university to form an equal partnership with the community, in essence, that they become joint stewards of the collected materials. The archival community has long recognized that ethnic groups are chronically underrepresented in college and university archives, but traditional models of collection development have not always been successful.[34] Many have taken Wurl's work to heart, employing a myriad of new and innovative approaches, concerned less with traditional models of archival endeavor and more with the empowerment of communities.

Participatory Archives

Several new ideas have emerged in recent years, including the concept of participatory archives, where members of the community work directly with the archives to document their history and culture. Using methods like crowdsourcing, archivists and academics are harnessing the power of the internet to create metadata for photographs, transcribing historical documents as well as bringing people together with common interests.[35] Jan Zastrow, in her article, "Crowdsourcing Cultural Heritage: Citizen Archivists for the Future," describes projects at the Library of Congress, Smithsonian, and National Archives which are democratizing the documentation process by drawing on the collective knowledge and experience of a population beyond archivists and historians. This new model for collections is not only shaping the archives but also encouraging communities to interact with the universities in new spaces.[36] The Grateful Dead Archives Online (GDAO) for example, invites fans to actively participate in building on and contributing to its content. "In keeping with the participatory nature of the Grateful Dead phenomenon, fans will be encouraged to 'contribute' their own digital photographs and memories to GDAO and comment on and tag digital content using social media tools."[37] Kate Theimer, a leading voice for participatory archives, has written extensively on the topic, both on her blog, *ArchivesNext* and in the archival literature. More examples of participatory archives may be found on Theimer's blog.[38]

Community Archiving

Another emerging trend is empowerment through community archiving. Realizing that community members and organizations may be unwilling to let go of physical possession of their materials, some institutions of higher learning have chosen instead to provide expertise and assistance to communities choosing to preserve their history in situ. Andrew Flinn has written extensively on this topic in several publications including "Archival Activism: Independent and Community-led Archives, Radical Public History and the Heritage Professions."[39]

For example, in 2010, the Denver Public Library, with funding from the Institute of Museum and Library Services, began a project called "Creating Your Community." The goal of the project was to create a digital space where communities could contribute stories and photographs documenting the history of their Denver neighborhoods. Users helped create over 100 communities on the site and contributed over 1,000 photographs, which are now part of DPL's digital collections.[40]

Still other institutions have focused on the collection of ethnic heritage using digital methods, scanning documents and leaving original materials with their owners. In "Beyond a Box of Documents: The Collaborative Partnership Behind the Oregon Chinese Disinterment Documents Collection," Natalia Fernandez describes the implications of the 'post-custodial' era in a collaboration between the Oregon Multicultural Archives and a Chinese stakeholder organization to preserve and make available cultural materials.[41]

Network Building

At CSU-Pueblo, the practice of joint stewardship has allowed the University Archives to make materials available not only for academic research but also to widen accessibility to a more general population. The Archives regularly announces the collections that it is acquiring through press releases, social media, and community engagement.

The Archives has come to realize how interconnected Pueblo is within the state of Colorado, specifically through its Colorado Chicano/a Movement Archives, and with other non-academic organizations like History Colorado (Colorado Historical Society) and the Pueblo City-County Library. The resulting network building is producing not only a formal means of access by the Archives, but also a more informal and perhaps more effective word of mouth exchange among members of the Pueblo community. For example, in 2014, a student worker at the Archives, José Ortega, a native of Pueblo with family connections to the neighborhood of Salt Creek, received university funding to complete a summer research project collecting and preserving the history of Salt Creek.

Moreover, the stronger relationships we have built with partner institutions (History Colorado, the Colorado State Library and the Denver Public Library), have led to statewide collaborations including: the Colorado Chicano Movement History Portal, an internet gateway to Chicano Movement archives in Colorado, and to the digitization and dissemination of Chicano newspaper, *La Cucaracha*, via the Colorado Historic Newspaper Collection.[42]

This example of network building illustrates not just the growing connection with the community but professional training for students at the university level as well. In fact, Ortega's experience in the Archives and his relationship with the community best illustrates how the campus is connecting with the community. In Chapter 10, Ortega reflects on his work with the community and in the Archives.

Throughout the book we use case studies to illustrate best practices for community outreach: how to network with the community to optimize collaboration, how to make the collection accessible, and how to process the oral histories into the existing archives.

Network building can also jump-start oral history projects. This happens when an individual or group in the community has laid the groundwork with an existing project, and has gathered a group of interested community members to form the core committee. Natalia Fernandez experienced this with the *Juntos* project, initiated by Oregon State's Extension/Open Campus program. The purpose is to connect the university and the *Juntos* program with Latino/a high school students and their families in rural communities and, through mentoring and financial assistance, to help guide these students through college. Fernandez connected with the coordinator of the program, who in turn, encouraged her to pitch the idea of interviewing students and their families about their experiences as migrants and first generation college students for inclusion in the Archives. Using this built-in constituency, Fernandez was able to create a focused oral history project in a short amount of time by building on existing connections. This experience made the community more willing to share their stories.[43]

Universities across the United States are turning to their neighboring communities as potential partners in conducting oral history projects. Students are also finding treasure troves of potential research material right in their back yards. Not only do these developments foster a stronger relationship between universities and the neighboring towns, but these new collections provide rich research opportunities for both town and gown, and a meaningful way for communities to participate in telling their own stories.

Notes

1 Stephen M. Gavazzi, Michael Fox and Jeff Martin, "Understanding Campus and Community Relationships through Marriage and Family Metaphors: A Town-Gown Typology," *Innovative Higher Education* 39, no. 5 (November 2014): 362.
2 Tom Heaney, "The Illusive Ground Between Town and Gown," *New Directions for Adult & Continuing Education* no. 139 (Fall 2013): 35–43.
3 Stephen M. Gavazzi, "Making Use of Assessment Findings in Optimizing Town-Gown Relationships," *Assessment Update* 28, no. 2 (March/April 2016): 2.
4 Ibid.
5 Oral History Association, *Oral History Defined*, Online, Available at HTTP: <www.oralhistory.org/about/do-oral-history/> (Accessed 2 January 2018).
6 Don Ritchie, *Doing Oral History* (New York: Twayne, 1995), 21.
7 Primary sources are usually referred to as eyewitness accounts of historical events or accounts that were created during the historical moment being studied.
8 Valerie Raleigh Yow, *Recording Oral History: A Practical Guide for Social Scientists* (Thousand Oaks, CA: Sage, 1994), 7–9.
9 Patricia Preciado Martin, *Songs My Mother Sang to Me: An Oral History of Mexican American Women* (Tucson, AZ: University of Arizona Press, 1992), XII.
10 Ibid.
11 U.S. Census Bureau, *Pueblo City, Colorado Population Estimates*, 1 July 2016, Online, Available at HTTP: <www.census.gov/quickfacts/fact/table/CO/PST045216> (Accessed January 2, 2018).
12 Dia de la Raza, the day of the race or of the people, is celebrated annually in contrast to Columbus Day. The event celebrates the Native American Heritage and asks for Columbus Day to be renamed because Columbus' actions towards native peoples were the beginnings of genocide. Cinco de Mayo is a day when the Mexican-American community celebrates its connections to Mexico. The event is held in one of the local parks with free admission. The festivities include Aztec dancers, Mexican Folklorico dancers, and speakers that talk about the history of Mexican-Americans in the region and how current issues impact the community. These types of events illustrate that the Chicano/a Movement is still active in Pueblo and show the connections to the historical past as activists from the 1960s and 1970s continue to come to these events.

13 Colorado State University-Pueblo, *University Archives and Special Collections*, Website, Available at HTTP: <www.csupueblo.edu/library/archives/index.html> (Accessed 2 January 2018).

14 Oregon State University, *Enrollment Summary*, 2016, Online, Available at HTTP: <http://oregonstate.edu/admin/aa/ir/sites/default/files/enroll-fall-2016.pdf> (Accessed 2 January 2018).

15 U.S. Census Bureau, *Corvallis City, Oregon Population Estimates*, 1 July 2016, Online, Available at HTTP: <www.census.gov/quickfacts/table/PST045216/4115800,00> (Accessed 2 January 2018).

16 Natalia Fernandez, 2 June 2015, interview with Beverly B. Allen and Fawn-Amber Montoya.

17 Oregon State University, *Juntos Program*, Online, Available at HTTP: <www.opencampus.oregonstate.edu/programs/juntos> (Accessed 2 January 2018).

18 Natalia Fernandez, "Oregon Chinese Disinterment Documents: Creating an Online Exhibit," Online, Available at HTTP: <ir.library.oregonstate.edu/xmlui/handle/1957/35839> (Accessed 2 January 2018); Natalia Fernandez, "The Oregon Multicultural Archives and the Miracle Theatre Group," Online, Available at HTTP: <ir.library.oregonstate.edu/xmlui/handle/1957/40090?show=full> (Accessed 2 January 2018); and Natalia Fernandez, "The Oregon Multicultural Archives: Assisting Communities Document Their Histories Through Digital Stewardship and Archival Education," Online, Available at HTTP: <studylib.net/doc/13841936/oregon-multicultural-archives-assisting-communities-docum> (Accessed 2 January 2018).

19 U.S. Census Bureau, *Boston City, Massachusetts Population Estimates*, 1 July 2017, Online, Available at HTTP: <www.census.gov/quickfacts/table/PST045215/2507000> (Accessed 2 January 2018).

20 Northeastern University, *Diversity Enrollment Statistics, 2016*, Online, Available at HTTP: <www.northeastern.edu/admissions/wp-content/uploads/2015/08/Diversity_OnePager2015.pdf> (Accessed 2 January 2018).

21 U.S. Census Bureau, *Boston City*.

22 Northeastern University, *Documenting Boston's Communities*, Online, Available at HTTP: <library.northeastern.edu/archives-special-collections/about/documenting-diversity> (Accessed 2 January 2018).

23 The Boston Marathon is an annual event, held on the third Monday of April, which attracts over 30,000 participants from the U.S. and many other nations. On April 15, 2013, two homemade bombs detonated near the finish line, killing three people and injuring several hundred others, including 16 who lost limbs. The "Our Marathon" project was an initiative to preserve not only the history of the tragedy, but to assist in the healing process for the city of Boston.

24 Giordana Mecagni, 24 November 2015, phone conversation with Beverly B. Allen.

25 Northeastern University. *Documenting Boston's Communities*.

26 U.S. Census Bureau, *Gainesville City, Florida, Population Estimates*, 1 July 2016, Online, Available at HTTP: <www.census.gov/quickfacts/fact/table/gainesvillecityflorida,US/PST045216> (Accessed 2 January 2018).

27 University of Florida, *Common Data Set*, 2016–2017, Online, Available at HTTP: <www.ir.ufl.edu/CDS/Main_cds2016-2017.pdf.> (Accessed 2 January 2018).

28 U.S. Census Bureau. *Boston City*.

29 Samuel Proctor Oral History Program, *Projects*, Online, Available at HTTP: <oral.history.ufl.edu/projects> (Accessed 2 January 2018).

30 U.S. Census Bureau, *Commerce city, Texas Population Estimates*, 1 July 2016, Online, Available at HTTP: <www.census.gov/quickfacts/table/PST045216/4816240> (Accessed 2 January 2018).

31 Collegefactual,com, *Texas A&M-Commerce Diversity: How Good is it?* Online, Available at HTTP: <www.collegefactual.com/colleges/texas-a-and-m-university-commerce/student-life/diversity> (Accessed 2 January 2018).

32 Texas A&M University at Commerce, *East Texas War and Memory Project*, *Website*, Available at HTTP: <sites.tamuc.edu/memory> (Accessed 2 January 2018).

33 Experiential Education is a pedagogical approach to teaching in which students use hands on or experiential activities to understand theoretical ideas.

34 Joel Wurl, "Ethnicity as Provenance: In Search of Values and Principles for Documenting the Immigrant Experience," *Archival Issues* 29, no. 1: 71–72.

35 Metadata is a set of data that describes and gives information about other data.

36 Jan Zastrow, "Crowdsourcing Cultural Heritage: Citizen Archivists for the Future," *Computers in Libraries* 34, no. 8 (Oct 2014): 21–23.

37 Grateful Dead Archive Online, *Website*, Available at HTTP: <www.gdao.org> (Accessed 2 January 2018).

38 *ArchivesNext, Links from MAC Talk on Participatory Archives*, Online, Available at HTTP: <www.archivesnext.com/?p=2716> (Accessed 2 January 2018).

39 Andrew Flinn, "Archival Activism: Independent and Community-led Archives, Radical Public History and the Heritage Professions," *InterActions: UCLA Journal of Education and Information Studies* 7:2, article 6, Online, Available at HTTP: <escholarship.org/uc/item/9pt2490x> (Accessed 2 January 2018).

40 Denver Public Library, *Creating Communities*, Online, Available at HTTP: <www.drupal.org/node/903926> (Accessed 2 January 2018).

41 Fernandez, "Beyond a Box."

42 Colorado State Library, *Colorado Chicano Movement History Portal, Website*, Available at HTTP: <chicano.cvlsites.org> (Accessed 2 January 2018); Colorado Historic Newspaper Collection, *La Cucaracha*, Online, Available at HTTP: <www.coloradohistoricnews papers.org/cgi-bin/colorado?a=cl&cl=CL1&sp=LCP&e=-------en-20--1--txt-txIN-- ------0- > (Accessed 2 January 2018).

43 Fernandez interview, 5 June 2015.

1

BUILDING RELATIONSHIPS BETWEEN THE UNIVERSITY AND THE COMMUNITY

While our case study institutions are located in geographically diverse areas of the United States—the South, the Northwest, the West, the Midwest and the Northeast—each school faces the task of determining the best ways to engage the community in an oral history project. Over the past few decades, these academic institutions created partnerships with the local community in order to bridge the divide between the town and the gown.

Here are six important principles that these university partners used when working with the local community:

1. *Understand.* Understand and educate your community and be educated by your community.
2. *Listen.* Involve the university and the community in a dialogue.
3. *Organize.* Establish an advisory committee and plan.
4. *Respect.* Build trust and mutual respect between the university and the community.
5. *Build.* Build on existing community archiving/oral history efforts.
6. *Communicate.* Address past grievances between the town and gown and continue to build pathways for communication.

These principles will assist the archivist and oral historian to better understand the communities they work with and to realize that the rich history of these communities is not just valuable to them, but also to a broader network of researchers, scholars, students, and the general public.

Oral history is a collaborative activity, where the interviewer guides the narrative through carefully chosen questions, but the narrators speak for themselves and are considered the primary authors of the work. The fact that the narrator is willing to share these memories should be considered an honor to the researchers. What narrators may not understand though, is how valuable their stories are to the historical record, how lengthy and important the collecting and preservation of the material, and how their interviews will be used in a research setting and the long term plan for preservation and use.

All the above have proved to be good methods for bridging the gap between the community and university. The university archives can be presented as a welcoming and useful resource, not only for academics but for everyone.

Texas A&M Commerce's project began in the classroom with the professor desiring to have students gain first-hand knowledge of the experiences of World War II veterans. The professor understood the importance of the war, but more importantly he knew that students would have not only book knowledge, but an emotional connection to this historical moment. He also understood that oral histories of these veterans needed to be preserved. These recordings were not just important to student learning but they had significance to the community of Commerce, the state of Texas and to the United States of America.

The previous section suggests ways to involve the community in a dialogue. Through this dialogue the university and the community begin to understand each other. The archivist/oral historian can explain exactly what happens in the archives, the importance of recording oral histories and just exactly what takes place when someone agrees to participate in an oral history interview.

At CSU-Pueblo the dialogue began many years before the Southern Colorado Ethnic Heritage and Diversity Archives (SCEHADA) or a focus on collecting the history of the region began. It began with the archivist Jay Trask and historian Fawn-Amber Montoya discussing the need for an archives that shared the diverse histories of southern Colorado. Trask received a Packard grant to fund the project and, through conversations with a work study student, Reyes Martinez Lopez, they began the Colorado Chicano/a Movement Archives. They visited homes of local residents involved in the Chicano/a Movement, listened to their stories and gained their support. Donations of papers, photographs and other documents formed the core collection of the Colorado Chicano/a Movement Archives.

The first step in bridging the gap between the community and the university is to find advocates in both arenas to talk up the oral history project, call for community participation, and recruit people to be interviewed. Natural partnerships and collaborations will emerge through this communication. Common goals shared by these entities should enable the archives/oral history program to grow its oral history collection, while strengthening its relationship with the community.

The partnerships that evolve will draw positive attention to the new project both on campus and in the community. As the word spreads about the project, enthusiasm builds, and community members usually come forward to donate their personal collection or participate as narrators.

It is inevitable that some obstacles will arise when groups with different missions collaborate for a common purpose. The community group may be focused on an immediate outcome—a book, an exhibit, or some other tangible item. The oral history program and ultimately the university may be interested in recording the interviews, preserving them, and making them available for long term research.

This is where dialogue is important, each group articulates its goals and priorities, and develops a working plan agreeable to both parties. Above all, emphasize the commonalities between the university and community groups, and do not let differences derail the project.

Joan Krizack, former archivist at Northeastern University, believes that pitching the idea of collaboration with the archives is a key to success with community groups. In speaking with an African-American community group about the importance of preserving records for future research, she noted that "one woman was really resistant, and she felt like the university was taking something from them . . . you have to present it as a win-win situation. We organize and preserve your materials, make it accessible to you and others and that's a win for you. They can't spend their time dealing with their historical records. They need to spend their time on their primary activity—helping people."[1]

A strong, long-term relationship between the university and the community is always a win-win. Such relationships take time, patience, persistence, and compromise, and it is always worth the effort. Oral history, also known as the people's history, is a great step towards cultivating these long-term relationships. Not only do community members engage as equal partners in the oral history process, but when the interviews are preserved at a neighboring university, the neighbors, children, and grandchildren of the narrators will benefit from the long-term community–university partnership.

Developing Your Team

An advisory committee composed of stakeholders from the community and university can be useful in designing the project, recruiting narrators with interesting stories, cultivating financial donors, fundraising, and helping plan and execute special events. Advisors are selected for their inside knowledge and networks for the project. They can then direct you towards resources and help promote the concept of joint stewardship of the resulting oral history collection. However, working with advisory committees takes time and effort to create an open dialogue where community and university members are both comfortable. There can be different kinds of advisory boards as well. Some advisory boards are set up primarily to advise institutions on the 'big picture,' as in the case of the Samuel Proctor Oral History Program. Their advisors are frequently scholars of national renown who keep them apprised of trends in research, or important issues relating to a particular population. These kinds of advisory boards are less tied to local communities as a rule, and as such, do not share the same sense of joint stewardship, although they may certainly feel it in a broader sense of documenting the community's experience.

In order to recruit an advisory committee, share information on the projects currently in progress. This can be through press releases or newspaper articles in the community. Distribute flyers at community events and express your interest in collaborating. Appendix C has a sample flyer that gives an overview of the program and encourages the interested parties to contact the archives.

At CSU-Pueblo, we set up an advisory committee of donors, community activists, and residents from various Pueblo neighborhoods. The committee is composed of six community members, the university archivist, one student, a history professor, and the Library Dean. Bi-monthly meetings are informal and the agenda is determined by what events, issues, and donors that the committee wants to discuss. The community members had volunteered to participate. They showed a special interest in making sure that the documents and their stories were not just preserved, but preserved with an understanding of what contributions were made in their historical context. This group understood why their stories were important and how activities of their communities had improved the town and the university. See the figure on the next page for the mission statement for the Colorado Chicano Movement Archives Advisory Board.

Texas A&M Commerce faculty expanded their place in the university through collaboration across departments. They empowered their student community who became the collectors of the archives and a sounding board for university faculty and staff. More advanced students served not only as mentors, but also as staff in the archives. Their goal was to understand those invested in the project as well as the complexities of the historical moment and the recording process. This student-centered learning approach made the oral history collection beneficial to students' long term plans, thus guaranteeing the longevity of the collection.

It is important that university partners understand their role and reflect the needs of the community. While the oral history collection will be physically housed at the university, the university partner still needs to establish a level of accountability to the local community. The university partner must emphasize the shared contribution and encourage access to everyone. This will also inform the narrator about how his physical items are being preserved and demonstrate that his oral histories are accessible.

Work with the community becomes a personal relationship for any university staff member or student. Community members are allowing you into their lives and into their private space. It is important to be respectful of these relationships and to communicate frequently so that the community knows that you value their contributions. While most agree that advisory boards are a good thing, obstacles may arise when trying to set one up. According to Linda Henry, in her article, "Archival Advisory Committees: Why?" it is essential to state the advisory board's purpose and responsibilities clearly in a written statement.[2] Otherwise, the committee may attempt to assume an administrative role in the internal management of the archives, or a committee may become a useless formality, wasting everyone's time.

Finding individuals to serve on the advisory board both at the university and in the community can be challenging but it also gives the directors of the oral history project a great opportunity to get to know their community better. According to Joan Krizack of Northeastern University, "we tried to get a professor who was interested in the subject matter and who was a member of the community . . . and who had some kind of history with the community—that was not easy

University Archives and Special Collections
2200 Bonforte Blvd
Pueblo, CO 81001
(719) 549-2475
beverly.allen@csupueblo.edu
http://library.csupueblo.edu/archives/

Colorado Chicano Movement Archives Advocates (CCMA Advocates)

The CCMA Advocates is a volunteer organization dedicated to preserving and promoting the invaluable history and legacy of the Colorado Chicano Movement. Members of this group contribute their personal knowledge and experience regarding the Chicano Movement to help guide the CCMA project.

The Mission of the Advocates: To further the goals of the Colorado State University – Pueblo Archives and Special Collections in acquiring, preserving, and making accessible records, films, photographs, and other items relating to the history of the Colorado Chicano Movement; in promoting the Colorado Chicano Movement collections; and in educating the wider community about the history and significance of the Chicano Movement in Colorado.

Specifically, the group will:

*   Represent and advocate for the Archives in the community
*   Assist the Archives to acquire important documents, films, photographs, and other records that are important to the understanding and interpretation of Chicano Movement in Colorado;
*   Assist the Archives to raise funds for the preservation and digitization of collections;
*   Help organize and volunteer to assist at events that feature the CCMA collections and educate the community about the Chicano Movement in Colorado;
*   Provide volunteer services in the Archives under the direction of the University Archivist

Organization: The Advocates will be composed of representatives from the community and the university.

Meetings: The CCMA Advocates will meet monthly.

Non-Profit Status:
As a volunteer group, this committee would not have any official non-profit status. Any funds raised could be received under the auspices of the CSU-Pueblo Foundation on behalf of the Archives.

Rev. 8-10-2016

FIGURE 1.1 Sample Statement of Mission and Composition of a Community Advisory Board

to do."[3] Because of the busy schedule of most professors, it can be difficult sometimes to find a faculty member who is able to participate in a strong working relationship with the archives. Much of the work of oral histories will lie with the individual that has decided to collect the interviews; this is true whether it is an alumni project or a faculty member having students collect oral histories.

At Texas A&M Commerce a faculty member guided the project and built the project into the curriculum, not just of his class but also of the History department. This connected oral history to research. This also created student advocates for the importance of the collection process. Interested students became the best advisors for the collection process. The faculty member was able to create a community of oral historians within the university community.

In order for the oral historian to overcome these potential pitfalls, it is important to have a timeline and plan for every project. It might be a good idea to have not only an advisory board but also a committee for each oral history project. As community members or faculty come on and off the advisory committee, a pre-determined plan will serve as the road map for new members to come on board. Communication is also key. If individuals are physically unable to attend meetings, they can contact the individual leading the meeting ahead of time and participate via phone or teleconference services like Skype or Google Hangouts. In this way, their voices can still be part of the discussion.

At Northeastern University, during the initial funding period when the major work of collecting ethnic heritage materials occurred, each ethnic group being documented had its own advisory group. After the grant ended, the advisory committees disbanded, and Krizack returned to relying on personal connections in the community:

> I would go to somebody I know and say, look, this is a really important collection for the university . . . do you know anybody on the board or can you help me out? So it really changed from an advisory committee to me calling on people in the university or . . . in the community to help on specific projects.[4]

In this way, she benefitted from the relationships developed through the advisory board even after it disbanded.

Natalia Fernandez, of the Oregon Multicultural Archives, does not have an advisory board or a committee for her collections. Instead, she serves on existing boards in the community to represent the archival voice for preservation, and to cultivate connections in the community.[5] This type of community interaction allows the university to gain greater insight regarding how the community works together.

Community advisory committees can be set up for many purposes—to help develop individual oral history projects, to develop expertise within a community to be studied, or even to advise the university. For all the pros and cons, when an advisory board does work, it can provide enormous benefits to the community and to the university.

Town–gown relationships come with inherent culture clashes that require patience, commitment, understanding, and time to overcome. This is understandable, since the two constituencies come to the table with different core values, agendas, resources, and working methods. They may come with pre-conceived notions about the other, whether implicit or explicit. Misunderstandings range from disagreements over financial matters to traffic congestion to safety concerns. A lack of understanding of the university's power structure may be aggravated by lack of communication between the two groups. Furthermore, universities are non-profits and do not pay taxes, and so may stress the town's infrastructure without contributing what the town sees as its 'fair share.' All or any of these factors can lead to pent-up or overt hostility.

So, how do the town and the gown bridge this gap and find ways to collaborate meaningfully? First, be aware of existing tensions and why they arose in the first place. Then be respectful and sensitive to the deep feelings of the parties concerned, even if the grievances seem unreasonable to you. Only then, try to find common ground.

A meaningful partnership between the university and the community requires trust and mutual respect. Find a neutral setting to explain how a university functions, what its workflow is like, and the uses you see for the oral histories you will be collecting. Then listen. In this informal setting ask about the history of the community, in order to find out the community perspective from the voices and hearts of its members. You may discover that the community version is quite different from your version, or from preconceived notions. Community members may also come up with ways to share and use the oral histories that you had never envisioned.

Perhaps the greatest asset the authors had at CSU-Pueblo was that we already had significant involvement in the community. The archivist formerly worked at the Steelworks Center for the West Archives in the Southside Bessemer community and the professor's family was from southern Colorado and her research related to the local area. While they were not represented in the history of the Chicano/a Movement, neither were they complete outsiders. The archivist was sensitive to the ethnic lines that did not get crossed; the professor, on the other hand, knew the unique character of the community. The archivist and the professor viewed the archives as a professional space while the community saw their stories as part of their personal lived experience. This left the potential for conflict or disagreement with community members about how to best process materials, what oral history projects had priority, and how much time could be spent on a particular project or community event.

Despite the fact that we were familiar with the area, this did not mean that there were not differences. Community members saw the archives as a means of activism, while the archivist and professor wanted to focus more on the oral history collection and the long term potential for research projects. The mission of the archives is to maintain impartiality in order to present multiple perspectives of the movement. This sometimes created a conflict of interest as the community members had a vested interest in advocating for their side of the story to be preserved, as opposed to perspectives from those they disagreed with.

When university faculty members are not engaged with the surrounding community, a certain level of distrust from community members may arise. The perception of being an outsider may affect how much community involvement and support the university sponsored project receives and how much the narrator may reveal in her oral interviews. Often community members see the university as an outsider. Narrators may also be uncomfortable talking about themselves, or in revealing themselves by discussing very personal experiences in a recording. It is the oral historian's duty to build trust between the narrator and the interviewer, and the university and the community whose stories are being recorded.

This idea of trust building is important especially coming from the university perspective because there are many guidelines from the university and changes in administrative leadership can create a gap in university and community communication. Gloria H. Cuadraz, in her article "Ethico-Political Dilemmas of a Community Oral History Project: Navigating the Culture of the Corporate University," identifies the complexities of negotiating the space between the campus and the community which is an important component of building that trust. "If my goals were to assist the community in documenting these oral histories, to gain visibility for the ethnic studies program, and to further my research agenda, then I needed to consciously navigate the challenges, remain true to serving the community, represent the ethnic studies program to the best of my ability, and remain hypervigilant about the design imperatives of the "New American University."[6]

In recent years, archivists themselves have begun acknowledging both the difficulty, and even, the desirability, of trying to maintain a totally impartial state. Even if we fully acknowledge our cultural biases, we are still biased to a certain extent, and this colors everything we do. In such articles as "Archivist as Activist: Lessons from Three Queer Community Archives in California," the stance of impartiality for the archivist is questioned and activism is promoted as a virtue. The article states that the archivist needs to understand the

> role of activism in the community archives and implications for re-examining the role of activism to incorporate communities into the heart of archival professional work . . . archivists can use this knowledge to foster more reflective practices to be more inclusive in their archival practices through outreach, collaboration, and descriptive practices to include communities in archival professional practice.[7]

Another means of bridging this divide is to employ university students from the community in the archives, as we did at CSU-Pueblo. This made it possible for the students to act as mediators because they are residents of Pueblo. It gave them experience working in archives at the same time that it allowed them to preserve the oral histories of their own communities. As time passed, the archivist and the student were able to collaborate on the collection of oral histories. Student workers were compensated with course credit, grant funds, or work study funds. Each year the archives recruits students who are interested in working in archives or libraries and students who are from the local community. This work has provided the students with hands-on practical experience in their fields of study.

As we mentioned above, each partner in the collaboration must benefit. Community members, for example, often want to see a tangible result as quickly as possible. One way for the university to build trust with the community is to process material quickly "to demonstrate that you're committed to the work."[8] A corollary to this, which should be obvious but often is not, is to be realistic about the scope of your collecting. It's often difficult to say 'no' but in order to be true to the material and have the ability to process it, care for it and make it available, recognize your limitations.

Furthermore, university partners should educate themselves as much as possible as to any historical grievances between town and gown, so that they can be sensitive to possible pitfalls. This can be accomplished by building relationships with the community, being aware of public relations issues that the university may be experiencing, and for the archivist in the acquisition and processing of archival material.

Community members do not wait for the university to take an interest in their history. Consider the example of the Lesbian Herstory Archives, begun in 1972 by a lesbian collective in New York City. The archives was a grassroots effort in which lesbians would collect, preserve, and make available to researchers documents relating to lesbian history and culture, while ensuring that the materials collected would not be filtered through a patriarchal or institutional eye. They adopted the following guiding principles:

> Principles: Many of the Archives' principles are a radical departure from conventional archival practices. They are inclusive and non-institutional and reveal the Archives' commitment to living history, to housing the past along with the present. Among the basic principles guiding the Archives are:
>
> - All Lesbian women must have access to the Archives; no academic, political, or sexual credentials will be required for use of the collection; race and class must be no barrier for use or inclusion.
> - The Archives shall be housed within the community, not on an academic campus that is by definition closed to many women.
> - The Archives shall be involved in the political struggles of all Lesbians.
> - Archival skills shall be taught, one generation of Lesbians to another, breaking the elitism of traditional archives.
> - The community should share in the work of the Archives.
> - Funding shall be sought from within the communities the Archives serves, rather than from outside sources.

- The community should share in the work of the Archives.
- The Archives will always have a caretaker living in it so that it will always be someone's home rather than an institution.
- The Archives will never be sold nor will its contents be divided.[9]

In some situations, where the community's distrust and feeling of exclusion by the institution is as deep as the foregoing example, it may not be possible (or desirable for the community) to forge a close collaborative relationship with the university, and this needs to be respected. There may yet be other ways to work with the community group, such as joint programming, featuring stories from the community archives. In the long run, maintaining even a cursory relationship with the group may be an investment in the future in the sense that community archiving efforts may be underfunded and ultimately unsustainable for the community group. In such cases, it has sometimes happened that community archives have ultimately found homes at archival institutions.[10] It behooves the archivist to maintain friendly relations and to stand ready to assist community archives as requested, but only if invited.

However, in order to work successfully with *any* community archiving group, "historians must shed intellectual arrogance which presumes that s/he knows better than the historical actors themselves."[11] Historians (and archivists) must also realize that members of the narrator's community group are the principal consumers of the accumulated oral histories. In "Oral History and the Writing of Ethnic History: A Reconnaissance into Method and Theory," Gary Y. Okihiro writes that the collection of oral interviews may also be the:

> first step towards ultimate emancipation; for by freeing themselves from the bonds of a colonized history, they will be able to see . . . their own history. From that realization and from an understanding of the majority group and their institutions, minorities can proceed to devise means for their total liberation.[12]

The academy can choose to respect the community's knowledge of itself, and adopt more of a stewardship role of facilitating the collection of interviews, as well as making the interviews available to a wider community and ensuring that they are accessible in perpetuity.

At Northeastern, as suggested by the project's title, the "Our Marathon" initiative with a focus on the Boston Marathon Bombing has primarily been community-driven, with library staff providing mostly support services. The archives' role to date has primarily been to help create structure for the project, and so they have created an oral history toolkit, including forms, interviewing tips and other materials for the use of those collecting oral history. The library's other main role has been to host the digital archive on its website.[13]

We discussed above some of the barriers to the university and community building a useful partnership, specifically trust issues due to misunderstandings, boundary issues, and general lack of understanding of one another. However, there may be other, even more serious and longstanding issues as well, such as the systemic and institutionalized racism within academia.

While an oral history project to document the history of your local community won't erase the community's historical grievances with the university, it may help to mitigate them or at least show good faith on the part of the university. For example, the Samuel Proctor Oral History Program did a collaborative project with the university's Theater Arts program and produced a play called *Gator Tales* which dealt with the struggle to integrate the University of Florida. The play accomplished one of the main purposes of theater; to make us take a hard look at ourselves and the ways we believe and act. *Gator Tales* was based on 14 oral histories collected from Gainesville's African-American community. The play uses the experiences of African-American students over a 50 year time period to put a personal face on the history of integration at the University of Florida. Mikell Pinkney, Associate Professor at the Department of Theater and Dance, commented that "there are so many people who probably have no idea of what it's like to be something other."[14] Actor Everett Yancy added "I want people to be humbled when they come out of this show, to realize that for just the sake of skin color . . . they could have had bad situations in life."[15] Program Director, Paul Ortiz stated, "rarely has the University of Florida ever been a positive tool for social change, so this project helped give UF a sense of credibility."[16] In essence, the project and the resulting play were not only informational, but moving and transformational for the audience.

Local public history work also gives universities an opportunity to come to terms with past discriminatory policies. The University of Florida, historically acknowledged as an "all white, male, Protestant university," has had a difficult time connecting with the African-American community, according to Ortiz.[17] The oral history program has helped the university to link more closely to its stated mission:

> The University of Florida must create the broadly diverse environment necessary to foster multi-cultural skills and perspectives in its teaching and research for its students to contribute and succeed in the world of the 21st century.[18]

So, the oral history program "went directly to the Office of the Provost and said that we need to invest in a project interrogating this. We asked for funding for it. And believe it or not, we got the funding."[19]

It is also very important to share the results of the oral history project with the public, both at the university and in the community. The East Texas War and Memory Project at Texas A&M Commerce has an ongoing lecture series to do so. Each month a veteran who has been interviewed comes to campus and gives an informal talk on his war experience. In addition, there is a Facebook page which shares the stories of narrators, students, and related events. This project enhances the university's connection to the community by sharing their stories online, at professional conferences, and in the local community.

When projects are completed at CSU-Pueblo's Archives, researchers may give a presentation on their research to which community members who participated in the interview are invited. Recently, the CSU-Pueblo Archives has begun sponsoring some of these events in coordination with organizations in the community. Events have been held in collaboration with the American GI Forum, the Pueblo City County Library, and El Pueblo History Museum, a Community Museum of History Colorado. These collaborations have made it possible for presentations to be given locally, but have also built partnerships in which the local library and state museum have been able to share information and to partner to create museum exhibits.

Travelling exhibits are another good way to present the oral history project to interested constituents in the community. Further, joint efforts with other libraries and archives in the area can expand outreach since you will be drawing on their audiences as well as your own 'regulars'. This will also provide additional media attention and excitement over the project.

As the university and community begin to work together, the divisions that separate them won't go away. Their complex individual and shared histories will come to light. These divisions and histories can be used as a tool to educate both groups to think about the importance of oral history collection both as the interviewer and the narrator. This will also assist them in discussing how best to proceed forward to guarantee the integrity of the interview and preservation process. The collaborative process, both within the university and between the university and the community, will enhance the experience of oral interview collection and will make the community central to the experience. This will help the university to better understand the history of the region and the perspective of their students and employees who call the community home.

Notes

1 Joan Krizack, 12 June 2015, interview with Beverly B. Allen and Fawn-Amber Montoya.
2 Linda Henry, "Archival Advisory Committees: Why?" *American Archivist* 48, no. 3 (Summer 1985): 316. (For an example of a mission statement for an advisory board, see Appendix C).
3 Krizack interview.
4 Ibid.
5 Natalia Fernandez, 5 June 2015, interview with Beverly B. Allen and Fawn-Amber Montoya.
6 Gloria H Cuadraz, "Ethico-Political Dilemmas of a Community Oral History Project: Navigating the Culture of the Corporate University," *Social Justice* 38, no. 3 (2011): 23.
7 Diana K. Wakimoto, Christine Bruce and Helen Partridge, "Archivist as Activist: Lessons from Three Queer Community Archives in California," *Archival Science* 13: 293.
8 Krizack interview.
9 Lesbian Herstory Archives, *Mission Statement*, Online, Available at HTTP: <www.lesbian herstoryarchives.org/history.html#mission> (Accessed 3 January 2018).

10 Aimee Brown, "How Queer 'Packrats' and Activist Archivists Saved our History: An Overview of Lesbian, Gay, Bisexual, Transgender, and Queer (LGBTQ) Archives, 1970–2008," in *Serving LGBTIQ Library and Archives Users: Essays on Outreach, Service, Collections and Access*, Ed. Ellen Greenblatt (Jefferson, NC: McFarland & Company), 124.

11 Gary Y. Okihiro, "Oral History and the Writing of Ethnic History: A Reconnaissance into Method and Theory," *The Oral History Review* 9: 29.

12 Ibid, 43.

13 Northeastern University, *Our Marathon: The Boston Bombing Digital Archives*, Website, Available at HTTP: <www.northeastern.edu/nulab/our-marathon-the-boston-bombing-digital-archive-2> (Accessed 3 January 3 2018).

14 Vimeo, *UF Gator Tales*, Online, Available at HTTP: <vimeo.com/119245728> (Accessed 3 January 2018).

15 Ibid.

16 Paul Ortiz, 22 June 2015, interview with Beverly B. Allen and Fawn-Amber Montoya.

17 Ibid.

18 University of Florida, *Mission Statement*, Online, Available at HTTP: <www.registrar.ufl.edu/catalog1011/administration/mission.html> (Accessed 3 January 2018).

19 Ortiz interview, June 22, 2015.

2

COMMUNITY OUTREACH

This chapter will address best practices for cultivating interest within the local community for collaborating on oral history projects. The relationship between a university and the surrounding community can be complex. The university may have pre-dated the community which grew up around it or the community may have been present before the university was built. As the relationship between the university and the community grows, a divide may arise between the two communities in regards to location, funding, and academic perspective. These divisions can make the community feel as if the university takes advantage of its resources without giving back. Although the university is institutionally stable, the community may yet perceive it to have a lack of commitment to the community due to the continual stream of programs, professors, and projects which may or may not have staying power. Furthermore, the community may not be fully aware of the academic research that is being conducted at the university. Since the university may be seen by the community as detached, wealthy, and rich with intellectual stimulation, many universities are faced with the challenge of how best to bridge this divide.

One innovative way that the university can better connect with the community and build a strong relationship is to create or expand the university's oral history collection to document the surrounding community. The community's knowledge of its own population can assist the university to understand the historical relevance of its regional area and will help the community see itself as part of a larger regional and national dialogue.

However, since a divide may already exist, it is vital for the university to consider the reasons for collecting community oral interviews. The university needs to consider what it can offer to the community and how best to develop and design a project that will fit the community's, as well as the university's, needs. Among the things to consider in developing a project are outreach within and beyond the university, cultural understanding, and presentation of research. The following are ways that the university can consider how best to meet the needs of the community:

- Arrange speaking engagements at the university and at venues in the community which highlight the role of oral history and encourage community members to take part in these projects.
- Attend events sponsored by the community and demonstrate an interest in its issues, history and culture.
- Understand that cultural differences may play a role in your relationships with community members. Don't judge, and cultivate patience as a virtue.

Outreach Events Sponsored by the University

Perhaps one of the best examples of CSU-Pueblo illustrating the work that is being done through oral history collection was in 2010 when the university's Department of Student Life hosted the Vietnam Wall Memorial replica. For two weeks, the replica sat on a large lawn at the university. As part of the programming, Student Life contacted the Archives to see if they would be interested in doing a presentation. In conjunction with the Chicano/a Studies program, narrators who had participated in an oral history project related to their military service and students who had collected the interviews in a previous semester shared their stories about the impact of the experience on their lives. The events were attended by over 100 people from the community and the university students (in their late teens and early twenties) discussed how the experiences of these men in their 60s had contributed to their understanding of their past. The speakers and the audience were deeply moved by the event. This example illustrated to the community the impact that their histories could have on a younger generation. University administrators were able to better understand how oral histories connect to student academic work, and also how the community viewed this collection of stories. At CSU-Pueblo, we have presented a variety of public programming, both at university and community venues. Students can also play an important role in community outreach and demonstrate to the community that community-based oral history interviews are a valuable resource for undergraduate and graduate research.

Outreach Programming Beyond the University

To address the perception of the university as aloof and uninterested in the community, make participation in community activities and events part of your regular outreach program. Commemorations and community festivals are key opportunities for university faculty and staff to show their interest and to promote the oral history program. It's also important that faculty and staff are able to explain the impact of the oral history project in their classes and in their own research.

Memory writing workshops and neighborhood presentations have become another popular way for CSU-Pueblo to reach out to our community. Recently, the Archives launched an initiative with a local museum called "Memory Writing Workshops." In these workshops, a particular neighborhood is selected and current and former residents are invited to participate in writing down their memories. Holding informational meetings with community groups to inform them about the work that the university has completed regarding oral history can also be a good outreach tool. These meetings can spark interest and serve as informal discussions to collaborate on upcoming projects. The neighborhood events are research presentations from university students who have used memory writing workshops and oral history projects to inform their research.

Faculty and staff may welcome the opportunity to participate on community advisory boards and committees or other significant participation in community organizations as another effective means of outreach. It can serve a useful function in making one more familiar to (and accepted by) the community. Personal relationships cultivated by these interactions are bound to build credibility with community members.

Promoting Cultural Understanding

Outreach and engagement increases the university's visibility within the surrounding community and in so doing deepens the institution's collective understanding of the community.

For instance, while collecting oral histories of one cultural group, you might be approached by others with families interested in their older loved ones sharing their stories as well. Keep your focus as much as possible, and try not to be led into conducting additional interviews which are obviously out of scope, but at the same time, it is wise to maintain some flexibility and be open to conducting an additional interview or two as a gesture of good will to the community and also to show that you do not favor one group over another. Try to tell as many sides of the story as possible—for example, select narrators of both sexes, different socio-economic, and educational levels to capture a multitude of perspectives on the topic. If the subject being documented is controversial, be sure to interview narrators on both sides of the issue. For instance, if you were to begin documenting the history of the Columbus Day celebrations/protests, interview narrators from a variety of perspectives. For example, interview Italian-Americans who gather to celebrate their Italian heritage and their ancestors as well as Native Americans who protest the celebration of one they view as a mass murderer of their ancestors. To interview people from only one side would only reveal one point of view.

Once the surrounding community understands that the university values the importance of its history, doors swing open for the university to collect more oral histories. For the Oregon State University (OSU) oral history project, collaborating with the *Juntos* project, and interviewing community members from farming communities in Oregon has allowed the Archives to connect with a diverse community across the state. This partnership has made the community more aware of the work of the Archives and they see that the university considers their stories to be important.

This flexibility should also extend to the interview process. Oral history interviews should take place at a time and location most convenient to the narrator and the project should be designed with a clear understanding of the time and scheduling demands.

Presentation of Research

In order to foster a strong relationship with the community, the university needs to be proactive in calling attention to the interviews to the local community from which they came, among students and faculty across disciplines at the university, and to the world at large. This can be done at a national level through research presentations at conferences, but also at local community gatherings.

Texas A&M Commerce, for example, has used these for scholarly pieces. Andrea Weddle, Hayley Hasik, and Jackson Dailey in their article "Redefining the Undergraduate: Using Oral History Projects to Promote Undergraduate Scholarship in the Archives," discuss the leading role students took in initiating the oral history project, locating and scheduling narrators, as well as public relations and marketing for related events. Student participation in oral history projects helps them develop their research and communications skills, thereby enabling them to feel more comfortable presenting at conferences and publishing articles about their scholarship.[1] Austin Baxley and Eric L. Gruver, in their chapter "Creating an Integrated School: A Divergent Perspective from East Texas," use information from oral history interviews conducted by Texas A&M Commerce to present another perspective on the integration of schools in East Texas.[2]

Information from oral interviews may also be regularly presented at campus-wide events that are open to the community. At CSU-Pueblo, we regularly make presentations at events highlighting our oral history program, such as Hispanic Heritage Month festivities or the campus visit of the traveling Vietnam Wall Memorial. These events get newspaper and television coverage which exposes the work of the Chicano/a Archives to an even broader audience.

Texas A&M Commerce has presented similar programming for the community, including a program where narrators were invited to the campus to speak about their experiences. This enables students who did not participate in the interviews to hear the stories of military veterans. In addition, by posting interview clips on their Facebook pages, this has greatly increased the exposure to students, university, community, and others.[3] Likewise, at Northeastern University, the community, faculty, staff, and students were invited to events where the opening of an oral history collection or digitization of a collection was announced and celebrated. This allowed those organizations which had donated their papers the opportunity to see the work that had been done, and also made other organizations think about their papers and the desirability of making a donation to the Archives.[4]

Building strong relationships between town and gown is a long-term investment which holds important benefits for both groups. Strong relationships promote better understanding of each group, meaningful cooperation and collaboration, and sometimes even economic benefits. It also facilitates the sharing of the area's rich history with community members, students, and other academics.

Notes

1 Andrea Weddle, Hayley Hasik, and Jackson Dailey, "Redefining the Undergraduate: Using Oral History Projects to Promote Undergraduate Scholarship in the Archives," *Archival Outlook* (January/February 2014): 3, 24.
2 Austin Baxley and Eric L. Gruver, "Creating an Integrated School: A Divergent Perspective from East Texas," *Sound Historian* 16 (2014): 19–30.
3 Andrea Weddle, 16 June 2015, interview with Beverly B. Allen and Fawn-Amber Montoya.
4 Joan Krizack, 12 June 2015, interview with Beverly B. Allen and Fawn-Amber Montoya.

3

FUNDING AN ORAL HISTORY PROJECT

This chapter will discuss how to fund oral history projects within an academic setting. It will include: acquiring funding, human resources, writing grants, tying your project to a specific event, and seeking donations at related events. This chapter will also highlight the importance of collaborating with departments on campus and/or community organizations to pool resources.

But first, ask yourself some questions about potential expenses for your own situation.

1. How many interviews do you plan to conduct?
2. Do you have volunteers or will staff be paid?
3. Do you already have access to recording equipment or will you buy or rent it?
4. How will you preserve the interviews for the long term?
5. What is the duration of the project?
6. What is your projected turnaround time for processing interviews and making them available?
7. What will your final product look like?

As you can see, there are a variety of questions to think about when putting together an oral history project. As you decide how to best approach the interview process, choosing high end on some items does not mean having high end for all of your project. The most important issues to consider are: What is the purpose of the interviews? What resources are available to you and what is the time frame for the project?

Student and Faculty Help

To a certain extent, the amount of time and financial resources that universities can spend on oral history collection will depend, at least in part, on the

TABLE 3.1 Sample Budget for an Oral History Project. This table gives estimates for low, medium and high end projects. Creating a budget during the early stages of developing an oral history project will give you a more realistic idea of what your resources will allow you to do.

Need	Low	Mid	High
Equipment	Digital audio recorder, Zoom H2n $200 Smartphone using video and/or sound recording apps $300–800	Consumer HD videocamera $1000–2000	Professional quality equipment 4K 4096 × 2160 $2500–up
Personnel	Volunteers	Existing staff	Hired oral history professionals, $200–500 per interview
Digital Storage	HD + Cloud storage $300–500	RAID array and cloud backup $1500–2500	RAID array, network storage and cloud backup $2500–4000
Publication Costs Costs will vary greatly depending on the type and length of publication	Home printer $5/ream of paper; $30–60 per print cartridge	Office printer .05/page Campus copy center .20/page	Copy Center (beginning @ .11/page outside printers; internet printers, i.e. Shutterfly, etc.)
Travel	None	Within the region—mileage, overnight accommodations, meals $100–200/per day	National and international travel Mileage, accommodations, meals, airfare $500–up
Training	Conducted by existing staff	Online workshops, or bringing in a speaker, $200–300	In person workshops $1000–3000
Transcription	Volunteers	Existing staff	Outside vendor $125 per 45-minute interview

Note: The above cost estimates are offered merely as a guide to costs in 2017.

university's organizational structure. First, do you want only to conduct a specific, one time oral history project, or do you want to start an oral history program which will be ongoing? The oral history program may be a standalone academic department within the college of arts and sciences, a program administered by the history department, or, more commonly, an initiative of the university archives, which is generally a unit within the university library. The size of the institution and the resources available to the oral history program will frame the type of oral history project that your university is able to take on.

The organizational structure can have a major impact on the degree of autonomy of the oral history program (greater if a standalone academic department, lesser if a subunit of an academic department or the university library). Likewise, the organizational structure dictates the funding the program is able to secure for its operations. If the program is a standalone unit, it will be able to determine its own priorities in terms of workflow and funding; if not, the oral history program will likely be competing with a raft of other priorities in the department or unit, and this may lead to delays in the process. Also, staff and faculty have many responsibilities other than the oral history project, which can interfere with their ability to focus on an oral history project.

To create an oral history program or courses that have oral history as a component, faculty and staff will have to prepare 8–12 months ahead of time and will have to negotiate this with peers in their program and with administrative leaders. If an oral history program or courses already exist, then this may take less time but there will still have to be buy-in from faculty and staff. With larger universities there will be more faculty and staff which may allow for some flexibility in planning for an oral history project. Of the institutions in our case studies, the University of Florida Samuel Proctor Oral History Program falls into that category. Proctor is a program of the College of Liberal Arts and Sciences which answers to the Senior Vice President for Academic Affairs/Provost, who answers to the President. The Interim Director of the program holds a dual appointment as a history professor and as Director of the oral history program. The Center however does manage its own budget and makes budget requests directly to the Senior V.P./Provost.[1]

In some instances, faculty may share common interests but they may already be committed to other projects. Good communication on campus about your subject interests may expand opportunities for collaboration. At the university there may be a culture of faculty and staff neither communicating about their work nor understanding its value within the context of their own university. If faculty contributors do not come forward for a project, it does not mean that they do not support the work; it may only mean they cannot commit to the full project. It is important to value any collaboration that can be forged in order to move the whole project forward.

Another great resource consists of graduate and undergraduate students, who are often looking for projects that will be completed in a year or less. This will allow the oral history program to have individuals willing to perform the oral interviews and have collaborators who are producing scholarship to share with the university and the community.

For instance, at CSU-Pueblo, we worked with a Chicano/a Studies faculty member who used the Archives extensively as a graduate student. For his work on Chicano/a activism in Pueblo, he interviewed a number of people who were active in the movement. Since then, he has expanded his research, and conducted more interviews which we hope to acquire for the Archives. When the archive or oral history program can work with individual faculty to promote the archival collections and encourage students to use the resources, sometimes a fruitful product can come about which benefits both.

Further, work study programs and student hourly positions help to staff the oral history program at the CSU-Pueblo University Archives. We do our best to hire students from the local community, and they have provided an 'in' to people they know in the neighborhood, both in terms of recruiting narrators and in helping obtain primary source documents such as photographs and other documents. Students enjoy returning to their community as a bridge between the community and the university and they understand that their community's history is important. It also gives them a voice in the long term preservation of the community history. They gain work experience for their resume and it encourages them to consider library and/or archival work as a future profession. This creates a mentoring relationship between the student and the archivist and/or a professor.

University Funds for Oral History

In a university, funds are allocated to departments and other units on a yearly basis. Units generally begin their budget planning process well in advance of the deadline for the academic year. After looking at the past year's budget and anticipating potential expenditures for the coming year, a budget will be drawn up and submitted to the administrator for approval. If the oral history project is not part of the current budget, be aware of deadlines and make requests for funds to support the oral history project within the required timeframe. A new program needs strong justification for the additional expenditure and this often means giving up something else to fund the new program. This scenario is becoming all too familiar in a climate of de-funding higher education.

Consider doing a pilot project that will illustrate the need for a larger oral history project. This will require fewer resources and if it is successful will make a strong argument for your institution that it should invest in a larger project. Sometimes, even when only minimal resources are available, it behooves you to jump on an opportunity and do a small pilot project using existing resources, in order to test your idea, pitch it to university funders, and to apply for sustainable funding for the project down the road.

For example, Natalia Fernandez at Oregon State saw this opportunity with the *Juntos* project, grabbed her existing audio recording equipment, filled up her tank with gas, and headed to a Latino/a community in rural Oregon to conduct oral history interviews over the weekend with some of the *Juntos* participants. After recording and making the interviews available online, she had a tangible product in the form of completed oral history interviews to help make her case with the library administration, and received monetary support to continue the pilot project.[2] The project "Latinos en Oregón: Sus Voces, Sus Historias, Su Herencia" is now accessible through the university's website.[3]

Find out if there is a contingency fund from which monies can be allocated for your project; if you can make a strong enough case, you may prevail. Obviously, if you control your own budget, this is an easier process, as you will be the one moving funds around to accommodate the new project. Planning for a new budget usually occurs one to two years in advance. An oral history project takes some strong initial planning and an understanding of a financial commitment to the project.

If funds are not forthcoming from your department or unit, range further afield and look at potential funding sources from other departments. For example, the Alumni office may fund special projects that help tie alumni closer to the institution, and an oral history project may fall into this category. The Provost's office may also make funds available for undergraduate research which might make it possible to hire students to work on an oral history project. Experiential education has become an important initiative for many universities and a program out of the Provost's office or a scholarly activities board may provide grants annually to academic programs which partner with community organizations to give students real-world experience and to provide personnel resources to the community.

If the project is of interest to the university president or to a university foundation board, there may be additional monies available. Pitch the project to your peers and your administrators. Informing administrators about your project will also help them to share this knowledge with the community members that they work with. A pilot project will give administrators the information they need to see that oral history is a worthwhile place to allocate funds and has the potential to promote the university to surrounding communities. Universities usually highlight the research that their faculty and students are performing. The archives is a space where faculty and students in the social sciences and humanities can go to conduct their research. Oral history collection provides the university a valuable opportunity to conduct research at a lower cost than lab equipment in the hard sciences and illustrates the value of and variety of research in the social sciences and the humanities.

Community Funding Sources

Universities often look for community partners who may have a shared interest in the material being collected. For example, if one is interviewing veterans, veterans' groups would be natural places to both recruit interviewees and to ask for financial support. Similarly, if the project relates to the history of social or civil rights movements, contact groups like The League of United Latin American Citizens (LULAC), the G.I. Forum (Latino/a veterans) or the American Civil Liberties Union (ACLU). For projects with a more general appeal, try the Chamber of Commerce and local businesses. Funding does not have to be through cash sources; it can be in kind contributions, such as gathering spaces or volunteer hours, equipment or the like.

At Northeastern University, the "Our Marathon: The Boston Bombing Digital Archive and WBUR Oral History Project" collaborated with community organizations and other university campuses in the area to crowdsource interviews, pictures, videos, and social media in order for Boston to share the experiences of those affected by the bombing.[4] The "Our Marathon" project included a large group of faculty and staff in addition to community organizations who assisted in the oral history collection and preservation. The radio station WBUR hosted interviews on their website "Boston Marathon Reflections" and the Boston City Archives collected the many messages of support left at Copley Square after the bombing. The collaboration received a 2013 Digital Humanities Award for Best Digital Humanities Project for Public Audiences.[5]

Grant Funding

You may also consider seeking grant funding in order to accomplish an oral history project, but be aware that most grant sources are highly competitive. Funding sources exist, from national granting agencies like the National Endowment for the Humanities to the local family foundation down the street.[6]

Many universities have professional grant writers or whole departments devoted to fundraising. If this is the case in your situation, be sure to work with these professionals. Many times they see opportunities in your idea that you would not have considered, or they see opportunities for multi-level funding in connection with other departments or researchers on campus. Some funding agencies, such as state humanities councils, look favorably on community/university partnerships. Moreover, grant writing is a bit of an art form in itself, and there are tricks to writing a successful grant.

Some general tips for successful grant writing include the following:

- Weigh the pros and cons of each foundation's requirements carefully. Call the grant agency, and discuss your proposal to get a sense of whether your proposal is one that they would consider.
- Read the grant agency's guidelines carefully, and follow them to the letter. Address all informational points requested by the agency.
- Ask the agency for examples of successful grant applications and check out the agency or foundation's website for lists of successful applicants and their projects

- State measureable outcomes and products—be specific
- Check your spelling and grammar—nothing turns off a grantor faster than a poorly written application
- Submit the application on time.[7]

Bear in mind that the competition, especially for state and national funding, may be fierce. It is important to be clear on what your goals for the project are, why the funds are needed and how your project will be assessed.

Most universities have a clearing house for grant applications. It's important to know what the guidelines are for your institution and to inform your administrators far enough in advance. If administrators are not aware of a grant and their signatures are required for approval, they may not support the project. In addition, consider the timing of the submission. During the school year, administrators are concerned with the multiple functions of the campus and a small grant may not be worth their time. During the summer time, fall and spring breaks, or holiday breaks administrators may be difficult to track down. It is always best to let administrators know that you are writing the grant and what the deadlines for the grant proposal look like. At some institutions when applying for large grants there may be more than one department applying. The university may not want to submit more than one application because they do not want two grants competing against each other or there may be overlap in the grant proposal. Letting administrators know when you plan to start writing the grant will save time and resources. If this is the case at your institution, administrators may have you hold off on your grant proposal or they may decide to merge multiple proposals. The Grants Office is also responsible for overseeing the number of applications an agency receives from the university. In some cases, you may not even be allowed to submit an application to a specific agency or foundation because it is someone else's turn.

If you are fortunate enough to receive a grant, remember that once the grant ends, there may not be as much enthusiasm for continuing the project, primarily because there are fewer resources. Set a realistic time frame for the collection of oral histories. This gives a funding period for the project, allows collaborators to see progress toward completion, makes it reportable to the university administration and makes it possible for follow up interviews as well.

When planning the grant funded project, be sure to consider ways to make the project sustainable when the grant ends. Even if you have a very targeted closed-end project that you do not anticipate adding to in the future, you may discover that the more people you interview, the more interest in the project seems to grow, and also the more voices, the richer the tapestry of your project. This is not to say that every oral history project should continue indefinitely. It is important to not unduly limit oneself by not thinking about how to make the project sustainable in the long term.

If a grant is awarded, remember that time must be allocated to deal with all the administrative paperwork related to the grant and creating new financial accounts with the university. Requesting time to work on the grant or writing into the grants a budget for an additional position may alleviate some stress.

Other Funding Sources

Do not neglect social networking and the internet as viable ways to seek funding. Crowdfunding is a social media tool increasingly popular for funding oral history projects of all kinds, including those which originate within a university. Crowd funding is a way of raising money by using your existing networks of friends, family, and customers, and by extension their networks, through the use of internet platforms like Go Fund Me, Kickstarter and Indiegogo. Should you decide to go this route, however, be aware that mounting a crowd funding site does require substantial thought and planning to yield a positive result. *Entrepreneur Magazine* recommends the following three keys to a successful campaign: 1) Research best practices for crowd funding and talk to successful campaigners; 2) Create a professional and well-designed crowd funding site, as this demonstrates your competence to complete the project you're soliciting funds for; and 3) good marketing in the first 24 hours to generate the most referrals to the crowd funding page.[8] And do not overlook funding through your own website. A 'donate' button is a fairly low energy method to raise money. Use Twitter and Facebook to send people to the donate button on your website or to your crowdfunding page. While online funding may be a great resource, it is important to discuss any fundraising initiatives with your university administrators to understand any concerns with tax liabilities and also to make sure that the university does not feel that you are competing with any of their other fundraising efforts.

In conclusion, funding oral history requires advance planning. Questions to consider include what programs or departments are going to collect the interviews, how can students, faculty, and staff collaborate, what will training look like and how will it be paid for. Leave no stone unturned in seeking funding for your oral history project. In these days of limited resources, when many nonprofits are often chasing the same dollars, it's important to think outside the box. Funding an oral history project depends on the scope of the work that you would like to achieve. Planning ahead of time and having realistic goals makes this much more manageable.

Notes

1 Ryan Morini, 26 July 2016, email to Beverly B. Allen.
2 Natalia Fernandez, 5 June 2015, interview with Beverly B. Allen and Fawn-Amber Montoya.
3 Natalia Fernandez, "Latinos en Oregon: Sus Voces, Sus Historias, Su Herencia: A Latino Oral History Project," Online, Available at HTTP: <ir.library.oregonstate.edu/xmlui/bitstream/handle/1957/59415/20160624-RBMS-Fern%C3%A1ndezNatalia-LatinosOreg%C3%B3n.pdf?sequence=2> (Accessed 3 January 2018).
4 WUBR is Boston's National Public Radio (NPR) News Station.
5 Northeastern University, *Our Marathon: The Boston Bombing Digital Archive, Website,* Available at HTTP: <marathon.neu.edu> (Accessed 3 January 2018).

6 Ideas for funding sources are in Appendix C.
7 See appendices for additional resources on grant writing.
8 Christopher Hawker, "The Three Keys to a Successful Crowd Funding Campaign," *Entrepeneur*, Online, Available at HTTP: <www.entrepreneur.com/article/234298> (Accessed 3 January 2018).

4

THE PROCESS OF ORAL HISTORY

Planning

As you get started on your oral history project, remember that there are multiple steps to take before the interview process begins. Good planning is the key to success. When the project is in its initial planning phases, it is important to think about the finished product and what is going to be done with the collected interviews. This chapter will address this process and give insight into best practices.

Decide What to Document

First, do your research. Where are there significant gaps in the historical record? Primary sources are fragmentary by nature, originating as they do from one person or one group's perceptions of lived experience. What points of view are represented and which are not? Many oral history projects have focused on under-represented groups, whose stories have often been overlooked. Further, many books and articles have focused on the broad history of a subject, like the Civil Rights Movement or World War II, but personal narratives can help flesh out a narrative, provide a different perspective, and tell us more about the everyday lives of those involved.

Ideas for oral history projects may originate at the university or in the community, and it is important for both to listen to each other. Not only will both have different ideas about how to conduct the project, but may also have varying ideas of what is most important to document. While an archives may be looking to fill in gaps in an existing collection, or to provide a fuller record of a topic, the community may feel an urgency to capture the memories of elders whose information will die with them. Negotiation will be required to come to an agreement on what the joint project will be.

Find Community Partners

To ensure a successful project, engage with the community from the very start. Consider organizing a public forum to identify community members with similar interests. The public library or a community center is a good place to meet. Also, publicize the project in the local libraries and historical societies. Your colleagues may know of someone or a group interested in collaborating. Utilize all forms of communication to reach a diverse audience: email, social media, public service announcement for the radio, an announcement at a local conference, and a university press release. You might even consider obtaining endorsements from community members as part of the outreach process. Even so, be aware that when you publicize a project before anything tangible exists, you may hear from people who have alternative directions for the project. You need to be ok with that and willing to collaborate with the community.

Define the project

The first step is to decide exactly what you want to document. Will you be documenting a neighborhood, a historical event, an ethnic group in a specific geographical area, life histories of community leaders, or something else? Is there a demonstrated *need* for the project? Write a mission statement explaining the purpose and need for the project, the historical background, significance, and goals. Based on the results of the planning process, write up a work plan which enumerates the tasks to be done and who will do them. Include a sample budget and a timeframe for completion of the project with benchmarks along the way. Consider a pilot project in the overall plan.

Much thought and planning should go into your project before it is launched. Do research to determine whether documentation has already been done. If some work has been done, your project should complement and supplement existing documentation, not repeat it. If no documentation has been done, such as in a new area of inquiry, like new farming practices or response to a natural disaster, partner with the community to survey the topic. Determine topics of concern and the questions to be asked.

Will the project be based at the university or in the community? There is a tension which can occur based on whichever approach you take. If based at the university, even relatively simple considerations such as the inconvenience of coming to campus may create friction for community members. Conversely, university partners may be anxious about ensuring the preservation of recordings created and stored in a community venue. Each situation will be different, and negotiation will be necessary. The university partner needs to educate the community on best practices for oral history collection and the concerns of long term preservation and accessibility, and the community needs to make clear its concerns about the control of the narrative, preferred venues for oral history collection and expected products.

Be clear as to what outcomes you want to see from the project. The community, for example, may have more short time goals in terms of outcomes, for example, an exhibit, a newspaper article, or a public program recognizing the contributors. An archives/oral history program is generally more focused on long term objectives, such as ensuring that interviews are properly cataloged, transcribed and made available for posterity. These differing points of view should be frankly discussed at the beginning so that both the community and university partners have realistic expectations of one another. Both the short term and long term goals are not mutually exclusive, and each stakeholder may need to make concessions.

Make a Plan for Dissemination of the Material Collected/ What Do We Do with What We Collect?

During the planning process it is important to think about the end goals of the oral history collection, how the information will be disseminated, in what form it will be viewed, and how long of a life do you expect the material to have? If the oral history is for the narrator's personal collection and to share with family and friends, then there should be a goal of a two–three week turnaround of an audio copy of the recording with a transcript to follow within a month or as soon as possible. This will illustrate to the narrator that you appreciate that they sat for the interview. If the final plan for the oral histories is to have them in an online exhibit or in a museum exhibit, dissemination will need to take place within a 1–2 year time frame. This will keep the narrator excited about his contribution and may serve as a marketing tool for the exhibit. If the interviews are being collected to add to the historical record and the goal is to preserve them for researchers, then there may be a longer turnaround time, and this may affect how they are collected and how they are preserved. All oral history projects should have a goal of long-term preservation, but project preservation may be determined by an archivist or oral historian and a repository's capabilities.

Memorandums of Understanding

One thing you may want to consider is a legal document known as a Memorandum of Understanding (MOU) between the university and the community partner. Such an agreement can help avoid misunderstandings down the road. In its simplest form, the MOU summarizes the basic responsibilities of each partner to the agreement, such as: who will do the interviewing, who will provide the recording equipment, who will preserve the interviews and make them accessible, and who will prepare transcripts and metadata. Depending on the complexity of the project and the amount of detail you want to put into the agreement, the MOU may contain other elements as well, including: a detailed description of the oral history project, a mission statement and goals to be achieved, and a timeline.[1]

Learn About Oral History and Oral History Techniques

Hopefully, *before* you decide to take on an oral history project, you will have familiarized yourself with best practices. If not, that's Job One before you go any further. Review the guidelines in the next chapter as well as other handbooks.[2] Take a class or workshop. For real world, practical advice, talk to other colleagues about their work in oral history. Colleagues with an oral history background can share their expertise and steer you away from common pitfalls. If you do not know anyone who has done an oral history project, consult the Oral History Association's website which has a large number of resources available online.[3] They can refer you to someone in your state.

One of the main reasons oral history projects fail is lack of planning, so do your homework, read about oral history practices, and talk to knowledgeable people before you launch into a project. Projects that are not well defined can easily get out of hand, becoming ever larger and more unwieldy, as word of the project spreads, and others not in your original list of narrators request to be interviewed.

> This happened to me when I did my first oral history project in 1979 on the Louisiana Purchase Exposition of 1904, also known as the St. Louis World's Fair. We didn't think we would find that many people to interview because the Fair occurred in 1904, and the youngest potential narrators would have been in their 80s. To our surprise, people came out of the woodwork, and it was much more than we could handle. If there had been sufficient planning at the outset, we could have arrived at a more realistic game plan.
>
> Beverly Allen

Write Up a Plan of Work

Define tasks to be done, who will do them, and in what timeframe. To this end, it is useful to create a more detailed timeline for the project with definite completion dates. Your decisions will affect the budget, staff skills, and outcome. Next, create a detailed budget to include equipment such as video or audio recorder(s), microphone(s), hard drive(s) or network storage, lighting setup, CDs and/or DVDs for access copies; personnel costs, including estimates for project director, interviewers, transcribers, editors/indexers, technical assistance with videography or sound recording, and people to create finding aids for the collection, create metadata and to mount the interviews online. You may also include cost estimates for travel to and from interviews, and for advisory committee members to attend meetings, fees for trainers and/or online workshops on oral history; honoraria for narrators and/or scholars to make presentations or participate in panel discussions, exhibits, and/or publications.

Name the Project

A name gives the project an identity and legitimacy and illustrates to the community and to university administrators that work is being completed and new projects are being created and completed. Named projects can serve as examples to grant committees of the work that the archivist and collaborators have completed. This also allows university programs, faculty and staff to be committed to a project and defines their labor in regard to the project as well as their commitment to oral histories. The community advisory board should be integral in the discussion about how best to title the project.

Create a Timeline for the Project

Setting a reasonable timeframe for the project, defining tasks to be accomplished in a specific time period, and the personnel needed to accomplish them, will break down a project into a series of smaller tasks, making a large project look much more achievable. As each timeline goal is met, there will be a sense of accomplishment and also a demonstrable level of accountability. The institution can announce the completion of projects and ensure that faculty, staff, students, and community members can get appropriate recognition.

A sample timeline for a year-long project is on the following page (see Table 4.1).

Select Recording Equipment

With the convenience and accessibility of digital technology, the day of the analog recording is, for all intents and purposes, done. Analog recorders, such as cassette tape recorders, have been replaced by solid state digital recorders. Solid state recorders have no moving parts and they record audio either into the recorder's hard drive or a memory card storage device. With the widespread use of digital audio recording devices and digital video cameras, files can easily be uploaded to hard drives and backed up without ever existing as a physical object.

There are a number of factors to be considered when deciding on the format of the recordings—audio or video.[4] The format will determine the kinds of equipment needed to carry out the interviews. While video interviews can often be more engaging, they require much more digital storage space than audio, and the project director will need to decide whether that kind of cost commitment is possible. Narrators' preferences should also be taken into consideration. Both Paul Ortiz and Natalie Fernandez indicated that they left the choice of audio or video interview up to the preference of the narrators themselves.[5] Not all potential narrators are comfortable being on camera, so it may be possible to get a better, more relaxed interview using audio equipment instead. Potential use may also determine the format of the interview. For example, if a documentary piece is expected as a final project for students, a video recording is more appropriate.

TABLE 4.1 A Sample Timeline for an Oral History Project. Remember that timelines are dependent on a number of factors and may vary greatly. Questions to consider: How many people will be interviewed? How difficult are they to schedule? How big is your staff and many other considerations? The above table is merely a sample, perhaps even an 'ideal' timeline.

Dates	Task	Person Responsible
January 2016	Investigate to see whether a similar project is being developed elsewhere in the community or the university; hold a community forum; find additional university partner(s) if appropriate	University project director
Feb 2016	Meet with community partner(s) to define the project—identify personnel, interviewees, equipment, and develop a budget, timeline and plan of work	Project director/ Community partner representative(s)
March 2016	Train interviewers, order equipment if necessary	Project director
April–May 2016	Conduct interviews	Project director and volunteers and/or work-study students, interns, class projects
June–July 2016	Transcribe interviews	Volunteers and/or university work-study students and/or staff
August–September 2016	Prepare metadata, finding aids, upload interviews to digital repository or other internet destination	Archives staff and/or catalogers
October 2016	Plan outreach activities; send out press releases about completion of project, and planned event	Project director/ Community partner representative(s)
November 2016	Presentation of project to university and community	Project director/ Community partner representative(s), interviewers, interviewees
December 2016 and beyond	Prepare articles about the project; plan other outreach activities	Project director/ Community partner representative(s), students

Also, if more than one narrator will be recorded at the same time, a video interview will clarify who is speaking. On the other hand, if you plan to mount your interviews on a website, and space is of paramount importance, audio recording would be a better option.

Digital audio recorders should ideally have the capability of stereo recording, using two external microphones (one for each speaker). However, in the interest of keeping things simple, you may decide on only one microphone. It depends on your staff's level of expertise and how professional a recording you need. The device should also be able to record in a high quality uncompressed format— WAV (or .wav) files at 44.1 kHz 16 bit and/or 48 kHz 16 bit—and have a USB connection so that files can easily be uploaded to a computer for long-term storage.

Digital video recorders should have an external microphone, preferably a lavalier or clip-on style which attaches to the narrator's clothing and produces better sound quality. Cameras should be able to record in high definition to the camera's hard drive or removable memory card, be tripod-mountable, and allow headphone monitoring.

Assemble a recording kit, to include an extension cord, extra batteries, tripod, equipment manuals, consent forms, notepad, list of questions, pencils and/or pens in a bag that can be easily transported. Include a checklist of its contents inside the bag. Establish a central place where this equipment will be held and define policies for checking out and maintaining the equipment. With the modern technology available, it may be tempting to use cell phones for audio recording but you will have better sound quality if you use an audio recorder because their microphones are made specifically for the recording.

Bear in mind that recording standards and equipment are constantly evolving. (In fact, there is currently no accepted standard for video recording). So seek professional advice before you buy.[6]

Select Narrators

Who will be interviewed and how will they be located and contacted? Oral history best practices encourage a project to include multiple perspectives around a topic and recommend that narrators be selected who can provide this perspective. The selection process happens in different ways. Sometimes many people come forward who want to be interviewed, and the project must be selective. Other times it is difficult to find appropriate narrators and the project team needs to cultivate more relationships in the community. Occasionally, people come forward because they have a certain agenda and see this as an opportunity to be heard. Other times, potential narrators will not volunteer at the beginning but as the project proceeds, they may eventually be willing. So it all depends. The project team should take all these factors into consideration when developing a pool of narrators. They also should consider the narrator pool as a whole. The composite group should be broad based and represent multiple viewpoints.

If you are documenting a topic or a time period, do some research and some networking to find those people. If the project is geographically specific, make a list of likely organizations, clubs, and individuals to contact. Visit local historical societies and libraries, and find out who is doing local history. These institutions will likely be able to suggest some potential narrators.

Within ethical limits use every source at your disposal to spread the word about the project and call for narrators. Word of mouth is a powerful tool. As the news of the project spreads, others will become excited about it. For example, at East Texas A&M War and Memory Oral History Project, after every interview, narrators were asked if they could recommend anyone else to be interviewed.[7] If so, interviewers asked them for an introduction.

Having a presence on the internet is an excellent way of getting the word out about projects. The webpages for East Texas War and Memory Oral History Project and the "Our Marathon: The Boston Bombing Digital Archive" and WBUR Oral History Project are excellent examples of the type of webpages that can be created. These pages illustrate the history of the project, collaborations, and have samples of the interviews that were collected.[8]

Put articles in the newspaper, on social media, and/or online discussion lists. At CSU-Pueblo, it has been particularly helpful to create topic-related Facebook pages to share information about oral history projects relating to the Colorado Chicano Movement Archives. It has proved to be a great way to publicize the project. With proper permission from the narrator, it is fine to upload clips of interviews for the community.[9]

Public forums and presentations in the community are also important for recruiting narrators. At Texas A&M Commerce, students presented their research to local organizations like Rotary Clubs, Indian Summer Days in Heritage Park, and at conferences throughout the state. As a result, project organizers were contacted by veterans throughout East Texas who were interested in participating in interviews.[10]

At CSU-Pueblo, the archivist or the professor contacts the potential narrator and begins the relationship. In the first conversation, which can be by phone or in person or occasionally by email, we explain the nature of the project, what is expected of the narrator, what the timeframe is, and answer questions. At this time, you can also assess whether the potential narrator is conversant and can represent himself fully and clearly. If it looks like a 'go', we thank them and make an appointment for the recorded interview.

At CSU-Pueblo our interviews are usually recorded at a location on campus. We try to schedule multiple interviews around a 4–5 hour block of time in order to set up the equipment. Grouping several interviews together not only serves our needs for efficiency but it also creates excitement among the narrators since they get to meet and share this profound experience.

Most narrators are willing to travel to campus as it makes the interview feel more official and they can interact with other narrators. However, in some situations, for the convenience and comfort of the narrator, it may be beneficial to go off campus.

On occasion, oral history may move beyond the individual interview to the narrators being two individuals having a discussion about their experiences with the interviewer. At Oregon State interviews were also collected in a group setting. The numbers of narrators present and their relationships varied—with family groups being interviewed, members of religious organizations, or focus groups.[11] The important thing to remember when collecting from or with community members is to be open to the format. Within agreed upon parameters, community members should be allowed some discretion as to the format for collecting interviews as well as the interview spaces. For example, having narrators participate in a group interview, or interview each other, may elicit a greater comfort level for them as well as bring forth information that might not be forthcoming in a traditional interview format. Although such non-traditional interview formats may be more free form and can potentially create some problems in identifying individual narrators in an audio recording, it is nevertheless important that the university and community partners discuss the pros and cons and have agreed upon objectives such as what questions are to be covered.

Arrange for Preservation of the Recording

Most of the time it can be assumed that oral history interviews will find a permanent home in the university library or archives. Permanent storage and access at the university is one of the most valuable benefits of a university/ community collaboration. The university provides the institutional stability for long-term preservation and archives staff have the expertise to catalog interviews and to make them available to community members, students, scholars, and the general public, online or in the archives as digital files and/or transcripts.

What this can mean to narrators and the community in real terms might include the following:

- Narrators can bring friends and family to visit the archives.
- Narrators can acknowledge that their voices have been heard and preserved for future generations.
- The community can see evidence that an effort has been made to be inclusive and to tell a more balanced story.

In conclusion, the process of collecting oral histories takes a time commitment and some long-term planning so include the community at every step.

Notes

1 See Appendix C for examples of Memorandums of Understanding.
2 See the appendices for further information.
3 Oral History Association, *Website*, Available at HTTP: <www.oralhistory.org> (Accessed 3 January 2018).

4 Doug Boyd, "Audio or Video for Recording Oral History: Questions, Decisions," Online, Available at HTTP: <ohda.matrix.msu.edu/2012/06/audio-or-video-for-recording-oral-history> (Accessed 3 January 2018).

5 Paul Ortiz, 22 June 22 2015, interview with Beverly B. Allen and Fawn-Amber Montoya; Natalia Fernandez, 22 June 2015, interview with Beverly B. Allen and Fawn-Amber Montoya.

6 For more information and specific recommendations, see the appendices.

7 Andrea Weddle, 22 June 2015, interview with Beverly B. Allen and Fawn-Amber Montoya.

8 East Texas War and Memory Project, Texas A&M at Commerce, *Website*, Available at HTTP: <sites.tamuc.edu/memory> (Accessed 3 January 2018); and Northeastern University, *The Boston Marathon: The Boston Bombing Digital Archive and WBUR Oral History Project*, Online, Available at HTTP: <marathon.neu.edu> (Accessed 3 January 2018).

9 Colorado State University-Pueblo, *Colorado Chicano Movement Archives*, Facebook page, Available at HTTP: <www.facebook.com/coloradochicanomovement> (Accessed 3 January 2018).

10 Andrea Weddle, 15 August 2013, *Commerce Journal* (Commerce, Texas).

11 Oregon State University, *Special Collections and Archives Research Center*, Website, Available at HTTP: <scarc.library.oregonstate.edu> (Accessed 3 January 2018).

5

THE PROCESS OF ORAL HISTORY

The Interview

All the planning has been done, you have located community partners, but you're not quite ready to start interviewing. You still need to recruit and train interviewers and transcribers on how to use equipment, do background research, compile a list of questions, and create a legal release form. The interview is the end product of the oral history process, and what most people consider the most rewarding. Don't jump right in. A good oral history interview requires training in interview techniques, a great deal of background research, carefully formulated questions, and a flexible attitude.

Selecting Interviewers

Oral history best practices state that the interview is a collaborative work between the interviewer and the narrator, with the narrator as the primary creator and the interviewer as the guide. The interviewer's position may seem somewhat unimportant but in fact, this role requires a great many skills—in subject expertise, interviewing techniques and listening. Oral historians acknowledge that the relationship between the interviewer and narrator affects the outcome of the interviews.

So who will do the interviewing? A town/gown partnership can usually find persons to qualify as interviewers among students, faculty or community members. Each group has specific attributes and skills that will contribute in a different way to a successful interview. For example, a faculty member will have the subject expertise to ask in-depth historical questions. The young student will bring a youthful exuberance and natural curiosity to the table. The community member brings the benefit of an insider's knowledge of the topic. Whether paid or un-paid, look for people with an open nature, and who appear as if they would be comfortable asking questions and engaging in a conversation.

Depending on the nature of your oral history project, it may be beneficial to consider less traditional interviewers. For example, if there is distrust for the institution by the community, one way to get around this would be to have community members interview one another, or to have a group discussion. For example, if documenting a community organization, recruit members of that group to interview others in the group. Since they were part of the organization, they will need less time to get up to speed, and will have a better sense of the questions to ask, especially follow-up questions. While some may argue that this may present too one sided a view of the organization, we would counter that oral history interviews, by their very nature, are subjective. That is why it is important to hear from as many voices as possible. Two members of the same organization may have very different views of its history and significance. To be sure, the interviewers should be trained in best practices, wherever they come from. A group discussion is more free-wheeling and less easy to control, but at the same time, that is one of its virtues. Narrators, who ideally have already been interviewed individually, can bounce recollections off one another, and often remember information that they would not have recalled in an individual interview. Also, with narrators who worked together in an organization, it can be very revealing in terms of the interpersonal dynamics of the group, revealing more nuanced information about how the group functioned and collaborated with one another.

Training Interviewers

All interviewers should receive training for the project. This way everyone, even the most professional interviewer, will have a thorough understanding of this particular project. If anything goes amiss in the interview, project directors can fall back on the training. Though initial training is most effective in person, usually as a workshop, it can also be done by videoconferencing or using a written training manual.

The Samuel Proctor Oral History Program at the University of Florida offers a three credit, 14 week course, which focuses on hands-on training in oral history techniques.[1] The course description for the Introduction to Oral History class describes the skills students will learn and a little of the philosophy behind the oral history program:

> While many still consider the academic study of history to revolve around archival materials, letters, newspapers, and other written records, the practice of oral history has steadily gained attention and practical use among historians. Recording oral testimonies allows a new window into the past, one that provides insight about historical time periods through the events of a person's life story. By learning about someone's trials and triumphs, interviewers are able to better understand past eras and movements through the eyes of an individual who experienced them first hand. Students taking

this course will learn about the theories of oral history while putting those theories into practice through interviews, transcriptions, and project presentations. The course will revolve around readings, audio/video clips, and discussions, in addition to field work about a given topic. Students completing the class will enhance their skills in interviewing, transcribing, editing, public speaking, community involvement, and organization.[2]

If it is not possible to provide such extensive training, at least ensure that community members and/or students have some knowledge of the subject matter and provide a boot camp style orientation to oral history techniques, such as a half day workshop. Such a workshop would include the following elements:

- overview of oral history;
- overview of this project;
- best practices for interviewer/narrator relations;
- practice in using recording technology;
- oral history interview techniques;
- doing background research on the topic;
- techniques for developing questions;
- overview of legal issues and instructions on the legal consent form;
- follow-up after the interview.

It would also include practical exercises such as writing a project proposal, plan of work, practicing with audio and sound equipment, and doing a practice interview.

If in-house expertise is not available to teach the workshop, there are other opportunities for providing the required training. For instance, Baylor University's Institute for Oral History offers several online workshops on oral history technique.[3] It might also be possible to bring in a presenter to do a workshop for your group, if you have sufficient funding.

Working with Staff—Paid or Unpaid

When planning the training, remember that not everyone necessarily needs the same level of training. If you have just a few interviewers and transcribers you will want to give them the full range of training, so that they can perform a variety of tasks. However, if you have a large number of interviewers and transcribers, you may consider specialized training based on their interest and abilities. These individuals can be university students or they might be community members whose histories are being preserved. If those assisting are from the community, that can be a huge asset to the project. Their knowledge of the community and their networks can make the outreach to the community significantly easier. Some may have a strong interest in interviewing, while others may prefer to work behind the scenes, doing transcriptions, or assisting with the technical requirements of audio and video recording. Others may enjoy planning special events, or have public relations experience. There is a place for everyone.

There is often a great deal of turnover with unpaid assistants, and when you have many of them to manage, training new individuals can be a drain on the project. That's why it's important to select individuals carefully and be upfront about your expectations and the nature of the work. It's not just about what *you* need; it's also about what *they* want. Organizations which do not make the work fun and satisfying will start to wonder why all their staff is quitting. So, take the time to adequately screen and train individuals to minimize duplication of effort. To that end, suit the task to the person as much as humanly possible. Give the potential interviewer or transcriber enough information about the tasks which need to be completed, so that he does not commit to doing something that he really will not enjoy. For example, explain the nature of transcription work, the level of detail involved, and the sometimes tedious process of listening to a phrase several times in order to transcribe it correctly. Ask about their interests and skills. Are they detail oriented, or do they get bored easily with repetitive tasks? Or are they, on the other hand, people persons, history buffs or creative types who would be happier doing something less detail oriented? What about schedules? Are they ok with a flexible schedule? Do they have a limited number of hours to work or do they want a full schedule? Can they work at home? If they clearly understand your expectations and like the task they are assigned to, it is much more likely to be a positive experience all around. Whatever their interests and skills, however, all should at least have a basic understanding of what oral history is, its significance, products and uses.

Students can make eager interviewers and transcribers, and they are in a learning situation as well so they may be used in a variety of contexts. These can be work study positions, students collecting oral history as part of a credit class or students completing internships or practicums. Whether graduate or undergraduate students, these students would optimally be history majors or students who are majoring in the social sciences (unless the project is strongly related to another discipline). If the oral history training is to be provided in a classroom situation, work with instructors to provide a practical experience for them, for which they receive credit. It may be better to have upper division or graduate students in their respective programs because they have had time to think about their major and have better communication skills. Further, students who assisted with the collection of documents can become community liaisons.

CSU-Pueblo has used many students as interviewers, either a work-study student working for the archivist, or as part of a class project supervised by their instructor. The student has always been a junior or senior who is interested in the local community and sees the value in collecting oral histories. The interviews have taken place in the archives with supervision by the archivist and occasionally with a class instructor present.

Recording Equipment

Whoever does the interviewing will need instruction on setting up and operating the audio or video recording equipment.

If the microphone is a lapel type, the interviewer needs to be shown where to put it near the collar of the narrator. If there is a handheld microphone, training should include instruction as to when the interviewer should hold the microphone versus the narrator holding it. If no microphone is available, think about where to position the recording device for the best sound quality.

If video equipment is used, decide whether the interviewer will be on camera or off. The interviewer should learn how to mount the camera on a tripod for stability and how to connect it to an external microphone. Instruct the interviewer to ensure that the device is charged and ready to use before the interview, and also to bring backup batteries and/or external power cords in case recording time should exceed battery life.

If the archives is making the equipment available to interviewers for checkout, a procedure should be followed which records the items checked out, and the condition of the device upon check-out and check-in to ensure that all items checked out are returned, and that the equipment is in working order.

Preparing for the Interview

The first step in getting ready to do an interview is conducting background research on the narrator and on the events that he will be discussing. To this end, we ask potential narrators to fill out a biographical sheet before the interview, so that we have some basic information about the person. There are certain questions we ask all narrators, but do not be afraid to add additional questions as seem appropriate as the interview proceeds. For instance, you might request additional information on something the narrator has said, or to clarify a point.[4]

The interviewer should also gather background information about the topic or event that is the main focus of the interview. For instance, at Texas A&M Commerce the oral history project emerged out of the analysis of primary documents about World War II and internships were created after students had some experience with the interview process. Students reviewed pre-existing interviews to provide them with context and spent several weeks preparing for the interview.[5]

Before the interview takes place, the oral historian and/or the archivist should have a discussion with the potential narrator about his participation in the interview and its implications. This is known as informed consent, and will be discussed further in Chapter 6.

The Interview

Decide how and where the interview will be conducted. Will the interview be done at the narrator's home, in the archives or elsewhere in the community?

The setting can affect the nature of the interview and there are pros and cons to every location. The narrator may feel more comfortable in his own home, which can result in a more relaxed and open interview. A video recording can capture a bit of the narrator's surroundings which might contribute to a better understanding of the narrator. On the other hand, the interviewer has less control of the setting and may have to accommodate for unexpected noise and interruptions from family members. A public space such as a library meeting room or even a recording studio will give the interviewer more control over the sounds, lighting, and other environmental factors, but the formality of an unfamiliar public space may make the narrator uncomfortable and less forthright in speaking. In any case a quiet space without interruptions will work. It is never recommended to do an oral history in a café or outdoor space.

Sometimes narrators have special needs that require close attention and sensitivity. In some cases, such as with the elderly, it may be better to go to the narrator instead of having them come to your space. In such situations, control the environment as much as is possible. For example, if the interviewee is in a nursing home, there may a conference room that can be made private and relatively quiet. If an interview takes place in a private home, ask if background noises such as fans can be turned off during the interview.

There is no magic length for a good interview, but in our experience, most interviews naturally last 45–60 minutes. Beyond that time, both parties tend to get fatigued and the conversation may start to ramble or peter out. The interviewer should be sensitive to the mood of the narrator and bring the interview to a conclusion when it seems appropriate.

Allocate one and a half hours if the interview is conducted at the university, and two hours or more if one travels to the interview. That window of time allows you to settle in, make sure the narrator is comfortable, answer any last minute questions, and setup and test the equipment. After the interview, plan for additional time to complete paperwork, photograph the narrator, and to discuss donation of supporting materials. Some interviewers provide the narrator with questions ahead of time, but best practices lean toward providing the narrator with general topics or an outline, so as to keep the conversation somewhat spontaneous.

At the Interview

Ease into the interview. While setting up the recording equipment, visit with the narrator in order to make sure the person is comfortable. The narrator needs to be relaxed enough to be open about the experience which they share. When interviewing people in their homes, a good way to break the ice is to ask about family photos and objects around the house, and chatting about other subjects unrelated to the topic of the interview. But be sure to make a clear distinction to the narrator when informal chat ends and the interview begins.

At the start of the interview, read a standard introduction to interviews such as the example below.

This is [your name]. I am interviewing [narrator's name] on [date]. This interview is taking place at [location; may include description, such as home of, office of] in [town, state]. The interview is sponsored by [name of institution] and is part of the [name of oral history project].

I wanted to confirm that Mr/Ms [narrator's name] understands that this interview is being recorded and that this recording will be preserved at the [name of institution].

[Wait or prompt for a response].

[Thank them for agreeing to be interviewed].

[Begin your questions].

During the interview, the interviewer can take notes of names and places used by the narrator, and check spelling after the interview. If you have an extra person available, that person can take care of notetaking freeing up the interviewer to focus solely on the narrator's stories. Even so, the interviewer may want to take her own notes of questions that occur to her during the course of the interview that she does not want to forget to ask.

At the conclusion of the interview, narrators should sign a legal release form which is discussed in detail in Chapter 6.

Follow-Up

Be sure to thank the narrator at the conclusion of the interview, and later, send a thank you letter, a copy of the recording, and/or a transcript. It is also a nice touch to fill out a certificate of recognition, using standard forms with presentation folders which can be found at any office supply store.[6] At the end of the project organize a public event honoring the narrators and acknowledging their contribution to the archives and to the history of the region.

Conclusion

The practice of oral history not only helps fill gaps in the historical record, but creates and strengthens connections between the university and the community. Oral history projects can create safe spaces for narrators to reflect on the contributions that they have made. In the case of students, they can learn more about local history and put the individual story into a larger historical context as part of their studies.

The time, energy, and money expended on an oral history project depends on how many people are interviewed, the topics discussed in the interviews, and how this material will be used in the future. Planning decisions, ranging from the questions asked to the kind of recording equipment used, will determine the quality of the result and just what information will be made accessible to community members and researchers. The interview serves as the natural bridge with the community and best illustrates the collaboration that is occurring between the town and the gown.

Notes

1 Paul Ortiz, 22 June 2015, interview with Beverly B. Allen and Fawn-Amber Montoya.
2 University of Florida, Samuel Proctor Oral History Program, *Education and 4+1 BA/MA*, Online, Available at HTTP: <oral.history.ufl.edu/research/education> (Accessed 3 January 2018).
3 Baylor University Oral History Institute, *Online Workshops*, Online, Available at HTTP: <www.baylor.edu/oralhistory/index.php?id=931747> (Accessed 3 January 2018).
4 Sample questions and biographical forms are included in Appendix C.
5 Andrea Weddle, Hayley Hasik, and Jackson Dailey, "Redefining the Undergraduate: Using Oral History Projects to Promote Undergraduate Scholarship in the Archives," *Archival Outlook* (January/February 2014): 3, 24.
6 See Appendix C for sample forms.

6

ETHICS AND BEST PRACTICES[1]

Best codes of behavior in the collection of oral interviews can primarily be explained through the ideas of the Golden Rule or Doing No Harm to Others. The ethics and best practices which should guide oral history programs consist in always remembering that the individuals being interviewed are those who are generous enough to share their stories. Regardless of which group of people is participating in the oral history process, a predetermined code of behavior for dealing with the group will not only enhance your relationship with the community, but will assist you in being professional when approaching any group. For best practices of ethics for oral history, one should refer to the Society of American Archivists' *Code of Ethics* and the Oral History Association's *Principles and Best Practices for Oral History*. These organizations have developed guidelines that, when followed, will assist the oral historian with a strong set of ethical values. These organizations can also help to guide oral historians when it may be unclear how to proceed, for example, in the event of a conflict or how to best frame the project to make sure that the rights of the narrator are protected.[2] This chapter will address ethical issues that may arise and will also address the responsibilities of the interviewer, the program and the archives within a university/community setting.

Archival Practices

Collection policies. The first decision regarding ethics that will arise in the process of collecting an oral interview is whether or not the interview should be collected at all. Consider whether the project aligns with the stated collection policy of the archives, if the processing of the interview will be completed in a reasonable amount of time and whether or not the archives can provide the access appropriate for the content collected. It is also a good idea to do some research on what other archives are collecting. If there is an overlap between what another archives collects and what you propose to collect, collaborate with the other archives to ensure that the scope of your project complements rather than duplicates the efforts of the other institution. Have an open and frank discussion with the other archives about setting collecting boundaries. It is also a good idea to check with these other institutions every few years to make sure that the collecting boundaries are still not overlapping. Keeping up with the literature and networking at archival and oral history conferences will help maintain awareness of what projects are going on across the United States and will also provide a venue to be able to share your work.

Conflict of Interest. In some instances, new materials may conflict with the mission of the archives or narrators may wish to place conditions on the donation which the archivist cannot in good conscience agree to, such as restricting access to only certain people or requiring that the papers be closed for an unreasonable amount of time. It would also be a conflict of interest for the archivist to collect materials in the same subject area as he himself acquires for his own personal collection. As an interested party, archivists may not provide a monetary appraisal for a donation, as this would also be a conflict of interest. If the donor wants a monetary appraisal for a tax deduction or some other reason, he should consult a tax accountant or an attorney. Alternately, the archivist may be able to refer the donor to a manuscript appraisal specialist.[3]

Interview Content. In some cases, the content of the interview may have legal and ethical implications, for instance, if the narrator discloses information about another individual which is of an intimate or defamatory nature. Revealing intimate knowledge relating to another person may be an invasion of privacy, and information of a defamatory nature may damage another person's reputation. In such cases, defamation could lead to a lawsuit, not only for the narrator himself, but also for the archives. While it may be difficult to determine how an interview could be perceived by others, the archivist, by having a set of defined ethical principles, can have a heightened sense of awareness so that if issues arise, there are guidelines as to how to proceed in an ethical manner. Because these instances will be specific to the archives and the interview, there is not one general solution.

Confidentiality. Confidentiality begins at the first meeting or with the first discussion between the interviewer and the subject. The confidentiality lasts until the narrator has signed off on the paperwork that states that the interview is available for the public. Until the paperwork is finalized, the circumstances of the interview, the names of those mentioned and the name of the narrator are confidential. In most instances, this will include the time spent processing the interview. This is especially important in community oral history where people working with the oral histories are bound to know each other. Ensure that all members of the oral history team understand this. This can become complicated as with community oral history projects more people may join the team through-out the process. The archivist may wish to give new team members a packet of information and have all team members sign a confidentiality agreement.

The Narrator

The narrator is considered the primary creator of the oral history. There is collaboration between the oral historian and the narrator throughout the project, with the narrator having final say concerning when and how the oral history will enter the public record.

Informed Consent. Informed consent is the process by which the oral historian makes the narrator aware of all of the implications of the oral history process. This information can be exchanged verbally or through a written document that clarifies the specifics of the oral history process. Informed consent ensures that the narrator understands that his participation in the project is voluntary, and details of how the interview will proceed. If the interviewer feels more information should be included in the document, she should make this consistent for all interviews conducted for the oral history project. Informed consent ensures that the narrator is aware of what the process is and empowers her to ask questions throughout the process. By having a signed informed consent, these papers can be housed at the archives for researchers and university personnel to be able to verify that narrators know that their history would be shared.

Narrator Safety and Privacy. If there is a concern for the safety of the narrator or for his loved ones during or at any point after the interview, the archivist may consider making the interviews anonymous or using pseudonyms. Further, the archivist may decide to provide audio only and to not provide any identifying information or photographs that might reveal the identity of the narrator. It might also be necessary to restrict the interview from access for a specified amount of time. The time should be determined by the narrator, in consultation with the archivist. In some instances, narrators will make the interview accessible after their death or after their children have passed on. Such considerations will provide peace of mind for the narrator, knowing that no one will be injured by his interview, while still preserving the content for posterity.

The archivist should also be cognizant of the wider implications of making potentially controversial interviews available to the general public. This may include political implications, public sentiment, and impact of the interview in the future as well as in the present. The impact may extend far beyond the archives and the local community, and have national and even international implications.

Respect for the Community and Narrators. As has been mentioned elsewhere in this book, respect for narrators and the community which they represent must be maintained at all stages of the oral history process. Archives must embrace the concept of joint stewardship from the beginning of negotiations with the narrator/community through to publication of the interview, and beyond. Institutions should realize that the right to preserve the oral history is a privilege being granted to them by the narrator and/or community. To this end, archivists and oral historians should make their best effort to ensure that narrators are fully informed at each step of the process, and that their input is both solicited and addressed.

Respect for Cultural Values. In some instances, the narrators may have different cultural values from the interviewer. Information may be collected that could be viewed as offensive by the community. Further, the narrator/community may have ideas of privacy may conflict with the archives' mission. Historian William Schneider, in his work with the native population in Alaska, considered these issues. In his book, *So They Understand: Cultural Issues in Oral History*, Schneider argues that:

> The archive is asked to be sensitive to local interests about how a recording should be managed, and to know the interviewee's and interviewer's original intent and sentiment in creating a public record . . . stories, even stories on tape, are not resources to be mined for information.[4]

In other words, the archives needs to respect the context of the narrator's original intentions in making the recording in the first place.

In some instances, the desire to respect cultural values and the narrator's ideas of privacy and disclosure may conflict with the archivist's responsibility to make the information accessible. In such cases, the archivist must weigh cultural sensitivity and respectfulness towards the narrator with the archives' mission and consider whether the interview in its approved form will provide enough research value to actually become part of the collection. Such concerns should be discussed frankly with the narrator and a decision might be made to not include a specific interview in the collection. Hopefully, such occasions would be rare, as these concerns should have been discussed with the narrator during the informed consent stage.

Legal Release Form

Narrators must sign a legal release form which gives the archives or the oral history program the right to publish, duplicate and/or disseminate the interview, including the right to publish the interview in an electronic format, such as on the internet. The agreement should also state the archives' responsibility to preserve the products of the oral history interview according to accepted professional standards of responsible custody. This form should be signed by the narrator and the interviewer at the conclusion of the interview.[5]

Institutional Review Board

In a university setting, at some point or another, you may confront the Institutional Review Board (IRB). The IRB may also be known as an independent ethics committee (IEC), ethical review board (ERB), or research ethics board (REB). This is a committee formally charged to approve, monitor, and review biomedical and behavioral research involving human subjects. The campus IRB derives its authority to review research involving human subjects from the federal government in Title 45 (Public Welfare), Part 46 (Protection of Human Subjects) of the Code of Federal Regulations.

In "Oral History, Human Subjects, and Institutional Review Boards," Linda Shopes offers suggestions for working with an IRB. Firstly, she advocates familiarizing yourself with the federal regulations relating to research on human subjects as well as the literature regarding how oral history programs have historically worked with IRBs. She also notes the importance of finding allies at the university who can help you develop an approach to the IRB. Since IRBs came about primarily as a response to the explosion of federally funded research in the sciences in the early 1990s which largely addressed biomedical and behavioral research, you may need to educate the members of the IRB as to established ethical and best practices relating to oral history collection.[6]

As of 19 January 2017, the federal government issued its final decision on oral history as it relates to IRBs, and explicitly removed oral history and journalism from the *Federal Policy for the Protection of Human Subjects*.[7] The exemption went into effect on 19 January 2018, and so removes the necessity for oral history projects to go through the IRB process in the United States.[8] For more information on the history of the *Federal Policy for the Protection of Human Subjects* in regards to oral interviews and Institutional Review Boards, Linda Shopes' article on the American Historical Association's webpage gives a thorough history.[9]

Access and Use

When researchers visit an archives, they ideally communicate with the archivist in advance to discuss use of the collections, either on site or through other means. This consultation is known as the reference interview in the library world, and generally consists of a researcher describing his information needs and the archivist responding by suggesting specific collections at the repository, and perhaps at other repositories as well. This relationship can be brief or extensive, depending on the scope of the researcher's project.

When the archivist grasps the researcher's information needs, she can tailor resources to the researcher's needs and possibly provide additional access or expanded permissions for use of the material. According to the Society of American Archivists' *Core Values and Code of Ethics*, "archivists promote and provide the widest possible accessibility of materials, consistent with any mandatory access restrictions, such as public statute, donor contract, business/institutional privacy, or personal privacy."[10] Oral historians, Barbara Sommer and Mary Kay Quinlan, however, note that:

> some archivists . . . approach the collections management process with a
> strong conviction that access to the material should be controlled . . . [and]
> that researchers . . . ought to be required to explain their purpose when
> seeking permission to use or quote from such materials.[11]

This desire to try to manage the use of oral history narratives by researchers after the fact, however, goes too near censorship for the comfort of many archival professionals. So, archivists may find themselves on the horns of an ethical dilemma in regard to two conflicting core values—on the one hand, the ethical imperative to make materials as widely accessible as possible and on the other hand, the ethical obligation they may feel to protect the donor from misrepresentation or exploitation.[12]

With new projects, the archivist/oral historian should be able to resolve this conflict by having the narrator review the content of the interview, and place restrictions on access at that time, if deemed necessary. In the case of legacy collections, however, the content of oral histories may not have been reviewed in as thorough a manner as it ideally should have been. In such cases, the archivist has a couple of options available to him. The oral histories could be reviewed retrospectively for privacy and defamation issues, and then the archivist would attempt to contact the donors, or their families, to inform them and come to a new access agreement. This will not always be possible, however, and in those cases, the archivist has the choice either to 'sanitize' the interview by omitting sections of concern, or to go ahead and make materials available on the basis that researchers may not take notes, may not reveal any personally identifiable information, and that they sign an agreement to that effect. Once the oral history has been made available, however, the reality is that archives have little control over the eventual use of their materials, especially materials which are electronically disseminated. Even though researchers are generally required to agree to and sign off on the institution's policy they may not always adhere to it. In such cases, the archives has done its due diligence and trusts that users will be ethical and follow the instructions of the archivist regarding use of the material. There is no guarantee, however, that even the best faith effort on the part of the archivist will not incur adverse consequences from a donor who believes that he has been misrepresented or damaged by the archives' access policy. So, it is certainly not a decision to be made casually.

Oral Histories on the Internet

The dissemination of oral histories on the internet has created controversy among oral historians. In her 2013 article, "Steering Clear of the Rocks: A Look at the Current State of Oral History Ethics in the Digital Age," historian Mary Larson discusses the issues surrounding placing oral histories on the internet and in essence, detaching them from their context. She notes that before the internet, researchers generally had to visit the repository. This meant that "practitioners could expect that very few community members would actually see the results of their work . . . there was much less pressure on researchers to be accountable, whether to entire communities or to multiple factions or interests within them."[13]

A narrator not being aware of how her material is used or how widespread the interview can be heard or seen protected the privacy of the individual and created a safer space for the narrator to be able to discuss her past. However, when interviews are placed on the internet, it opens them up to a much broader audience, "those who participated and those who did not, those who were interested at the time and those who were not, those who agreed with the project and those who did not."[14] When people of varying perspectives in the community become aware of these resources, it can become a hot potato for the institution and give rise to a sense of having a trust broken between the community and the university.

It may also have repercussions for researchers who are made forcibly aware of how their work may be regarded by the communities they studied. This is not necessarily a bad thing as it will make them more accountable to the community and more intentional about how they approach their work.[15] Some researchers are able to make the adjustment, but others may find the potential for backlash too great and decide not to make their work available on the internet.[16]

An oral interview housed in an archives where someone had to fill out a registration form, show identification, and thereby be given permission to see the transcript or to hear the audio meant that there was some level of protection for the narrator. In the digital age, researchers, archivists, and interviewers need to take greater considerations for how this information can be used (or potentially misused). Larson argues that the narrator will become more of a joint steward of the materials. This can have benefits for both the narrator and the archives. As a result of doing the interview, the narrator may donate additional materials and/or recruit other donors to do the same. The narrator may also be moved to serve as a consultant, giving archivists and researchers another perspective from which to better understand the communities whose histories they are interested in preserving. This may result in the archives becoming more community focused and perhaps less researcher driven, in the sense of being simply mined for information.[17]

For narrators whose interviews may be personally damaging, give a harsh view of the community, or frame others in a negative light, the archivist needs to remember to be accountable to ideas of privacy and may decide to not make these interviews accessible online. When the narrator signs the release, he should be made aware that his material may be placed in a digital format and made broadly accessible. The archivist, by being connected to the community, will understand the context for the interview and will decide, in consultation with the narrator, and sometimes an entire community, what should be made accessible.

Hard Questions

Hard questions that have no clear answers arise in every oral history project, and probably more than ever in university/community relations. Here are some areas in which problems may arise.

Getting Communities to Agree

One of the keys to creating a successful collaboration involves the attitude of university partners to their community counterparts. Both should participate in the planning of the project, and respect one another's viewpoints and suggestions. University partners should realize that there may be negotiations involved in getting both parties to agree to certain points of the project. And get it in writing!

Meeting Communities on their Own Turf

Another point to consider, which may seem trivial at first, is to meet at community venues as well as university ones. Not only is this more fair and convenient for all, but also an excellent way for the university partner to become more visible in the community. This also allows for the university to come to a better understanding of the needs of the community in regards to accessing buildings, but also understand that not all community members feel welcome at the university.

University Administration Conflicts

It will come as no surprise that at times, the university partner may be thwarted from within in its goals for the project. Not only do departmental priorities change from time to time, but budgets are also subject to cutting by the administrative unit within which the archives exists. These sorts of conflicts are out of the control of the archives or oral history program, but can seriously undercut effectiveness, to say nothing of damaging public relations. To combat this sort of conflict, continually try to show the administration tangible benefits of the project, for example, better community relations, and increased educational opportunities for students in increased educational opportunities.

Ensuring both University and Community Partners Live Up to their Responsibilities

Community members need to see that their participation in the project is beneficial to them, not only to the university. Tangible products, such as transcribed interviews and public events celebrating those products, can help with this. On the other hand, community partners' support is essential to the success of the project. However, commitments such as providing volunteer assistance for transcribing, interviewing and other tasks, as well as promised financial commitments can be hard for outside partners to be able to complete. As always, creating and cultivating good will, by such means as attending community events, serving on local boards and generally being willing to go out into the community, can generate goodwill for the university partner.

Conclusion

Ethical questions are not easily answered and require some type of professional perspective to address. These questions may arise when considering the best interests of the community or the individual, the university or the narrator, or the researcher and the archivist. The question at the heart of ethical ideas for oral history collection is "What is the purpose of the oral history?" Archivists, as stewards of history and cultural heritage, need to understand best practices in their profession, show compassion, be willing to listen, and use a perspective that understands the past, has a desire to accurately reflect the present, and makes sure the information is available in the future.

Notes

1 Adapted from: Nancy MacKay, *Curating Oral Histories: From Interview to Archive*, "Chapter 5. Ethical Considerations," 2nd ed. (New York: Routledge, 2016).
2 Oral History Association, *Principles and Best Practices*, Online, Available at HTTP: <www.oralhistory.org/about/principles-and-practices/> (Accessed 3 January 2018).
3 Society of American Archivists, *Donating your Personal or Family Papers to a Repository*, Online, Available at HTTP: <www2.archivists.org/publications/brochures/donating-familyrecs> (Accessed 3 January 2018).
4 William Schneider, *So They Understand: Cultural Issues in Oral History* (Logan, UT: Utah State University Press, 2002), 151–152.
5 For an example of an oral history release form, see Appendix C.
6 Linda Shopes, "Oral History, Human Subjects and Institutional Review Boards," Online, Available at HTTP: <www.oralhistory.org/about/do-oral-history/oral-history-and-irb-review/> (Accessed 3 January 2018).
7 U.S. Department of Health and Human Services, *Federal Policy for the Protection of Human Subjects ('Common Rule')*, Online, Available at HTTP: <www.hhs.gov/ohrp/regulations-and-policy/regulations/common-rule/> (Accessed 3 January 2018).
8 National Coalition for History, *New Federal Rule Exempts Oral History From IRB Review*, Online, Available at HTTP: <historycoalition.org/2017/01/19/new-federal-rule-exempts-oral-history-from-irb-review/> (Accessed 3 January 2018).
9 Linda Shopes, "Negotiating Institutional Review Boards," Online, Available at HTTP: <www.historians.org/publications-and-directories/perspectives-on-history/march-2007/institutional-review-boards> (Accessed 3 January 2018).
10 Society of American Archivists, *SAA Core Values Statement and Code of Ethics*, Online, Available at HTTP: <www2.archivists.org/statements/saa-core-values-statement-and-code-of-ethics> (Accessed 3 January 2018).
11 Barbara W. Sommer and Mary Kay Quinlan, *The Oral History Manual*, 2nd ed. (Lanham, MD: Altamira Press, 2009), 28.
12 Ibid.
13 Mary A. Larson, "Steering Clear of the Rocks: A Look at the Current State of Oral History Ethics in the Digital Age," *The Oral History Review* 40, no. 1 (2013): 46.
14 Ibid.
15 Ibid.
16 Ibid.
17 Schneider, *So They Understand*, 151–152.

7

TELLING THE WORLD

Sharing the Project and Making it Accessible to the Community

Once the project has been completed, the first priority is to announce it. Do this as soon as practical, while the energy is high and most of the participants are around and willing to participate.

Sharing the Project

You could do this in a number of ways—having an official 'opening' of the collection and announcing it in press releases, hosting an event, or creating an exhibit based on the oral histories. It is essential that narrators, interviewers, and project volunteers be publicly acknowledged. If the project is well designed, executed and presented, its value will be self-evident to funders, potential researchers and other stakeholders. Narrators can take pride in their contribution to local history and funders will see that their money has been used wisely to produce a quality product. Researchers will discover a new primary source to supplement their own work.

Do not neglect social networking as a means to spread the word. Create a Facebook page, as we did for the Colorado Chicano/a Movement Archives at CSU-Pueblo. On the Facebook page, share news and excerpts from interviews and invite 'friends' to share their recollections as well. Posting on social media can lead you to potential donors as well as potential narrators. A Facebook page requires less maintenance than a website—it can be easily updated and managed by a volunteer. Facebook also allows you to create event pages in which invitations can be shared electronically.[1]

There are other ways of bringing attention to the project, such as a public event in which you highlight the interviews at a reception in the community. You might also present mini-documentaries using clips in a presentation to the university community. Traveling exhibits showing the results of the project can also move from one place to another in the community—shopping malls, community centers, and public library branches are just a few examples.

Do not forget the more traditional means of getting the word out—press releases, announcements in relevant trade publications, and presentations to both professional groups and community groups.

Local or national holidays or festivals offer a great opportunity to promote the project. A table at a festival, a reading or performance, or simply handing out a brochure can reach a large number of people at a ready-made event. If your interviews contain a large number of military veterans, then Memorial Day and Veteran's Day are good times to discuss the project. If your interviews focus on ethnic heritage, then perhaps Hispanic Heritage Month, Black History Month, Asian-American/Pacific Islander, and/or Native American History Month might be good times to share the project. This gives the university an event to highlight to the community. If campus events are scheduled for ethnic heritage months, join a planning committee to advocate for an oral history table. If these events are held annually, it is easy to use materials, or at least ideas, from one year to the next. It might even be possible to develop an oral history project around an ethnic heritage festival and to partner with other programs or departments on campus for getting interviews.

Making Interviews Available

Once the oral history project is finished, interviews should be made available to the local and scholarly community for research and general enjoyment. Most archives have a reading room where users can read/view/listen to the interviews in the archives. For more distant users, most archives today make interviews available in some form on the internet.

Here are a number of tools that libraries and archives use to increase access to the *content* of interviews. Depending on your resources, that 'access' can take a variety of forms.

Catalog records: The most basic level of access would be a description of an individual interview, which might take the form of a *catalog record*. Many university libraries have cataloging departments where skilled catalogers can create an electronic record for the interview based on information provided by the oral historian. Catalog records contain basic information about the oral history such as names of narrator and interviewer, interview title, description of the content of the interview, name of the oral history project, dates the interviews were conducted, and sometimes subject descriptors.[2]

Finding aid: According to the Society of American Archivists website a finding aid is:

1. A tool that facilitates discovery of information within a collection of records.

2. A description of records that gives the repository physical and intellectual control over the materials and that assists users to gain access to and understand the materials.[3]

You might also want to consider doing one of the following descriptive records instead of, or in addition to a catalog record.

In general, finding aids are created for a collection of oral histories, and not for one individual oral history. If you have described your oral histories on an item level, that is the ideal, since it will be most helpful to researchers. Many institutions, however, have legacy collections of oral histories which have not been described to that level. For those, a finding aid, with a listing of narrators, dates, or whatever basic information you have on the item level will provide basic access, and you may be able to do item level descriptions at some later date.

Online catalogs: You can also submit descriptions of your holdings to online combined catalogs which describe the collections of a number of libraries. Some of these catalogs, like OCLC's ArchiveGrid, are free; others, like OCLC's WorldCat, are fee based.[4]

Indexes and Transcriptions: If you have prepared indexes and/or transcriptions of the interviews, they can be hyperlinked to the appropriate catalog record. Alternatively, indexes and transcriptions can be uploaded to an existing website.

In some instances community members or researchers may want copies of the interviews or of the transcriptions. Project directors need to decide if these will be given to anyone who asks or what policies the archives will have for access. In addition, they will need to decide how they will transfer the material to the individual asking. Will this be in the form of a DVD or a digital audio file? The project directors need to decide if there will be a cost for individuals to be able to access the entire interview or to get a copy of it. Most archives will provide copies of the interview for narrators, but will charge researchers a processing fee and the cost of the DVD and postage.

Streaming Audio and Video

There are multiple options for making oral histories available online via streaming audio and/or video. Some are relatively inexpensive, while others may be prohibitively expensive, depending on your situation. Of course, there are tradeoffs in either scenario.

Sometimes the quickest approach is to upload interviews, or clips of longer interviews, to non-profit hosting services like Internet Archive or ITunes University, or commercial services like YouTube and Vimeo. These are no-cost or low-cost alternatives, but be sure to check terms of service agreements *very* carefully to learn what rights you may be giving up by using a third party provider. For example, although YouTube affirms that you retain all ownership rights to your content, nevertheless, by virtue of uploading that content, you grant YouTube a:

worldwide, non-exclusive, royalty-free, sublicenseable and transferable license to use, reproduce, distribute, prepare derivative works of display . . . including without limitation for promoting and redistributing part or all of the Service (and derivative works thereof) in any media formats and through any media channels.[5]

In essence, you are giving up your exclusive copyright in the material. We do not generally recommend this route as the best option for disseminating your materials. However, if you have no other means of making the material available to as wide a public as possible, you may decide that the sacrifice is worthwhile. Just be aware of what you may be giving up. It is also important to become familiar with what your institution's policy is on posting digital content on third party websites, especially if there are issues regarding copyright.

You can host the streaming media yourself, or outsource it; both require substantial investments of time and money. To host it yourself requires a robust web platform with lots of bandwidth, digital library software, and a high-level IT staff person to administer it. This is common at larger universities. A digital library (also referred to as a digital repository) is an electronic library with a focused collection of digital objects that can include text, still photos, audio and video recordings, all stored as electronic media formats. Examples include commercial software programs that work in digital libraries like Content DM, or open source alternatives like DSpace or Drupal.[6] Many universities have created digital repositories or have access to them through consortial agreements with other libraries in their region, so check to see if you may already have access to an existing digital repository.

Smaller institutions may prefer to partner with another institution which has an existing digital repository and can provide the expertise and support for digital preservation. It is also possible that your regional oral history association or large public library may have established a digital repository into which you can deposit interviews for a fee that is less than the cost of digital storage and maintenance.

The Digital Public Library of America (DPLA) is a relatively new option that you may want to investigate. DPLA is a portal which both contains and points to digital objects from libraries across America, in essence a combined libraries digital object browser. Libraries can participate by joining a state or regional 'hub', and submitting their digital objects to the hub for addition to the database. This may be a good option for smaller libraries that do not have sufficient IT staff to manage a digital repository. As DPLA is very new, there may not be a hub in your area yet, but there probably soon will be.[7]

Streaming media can also be outsourced and hosted at third party sites, such as Kaltura Mediaspace, a social video and rich media portal which you can link to from your website.[8] With Kaltura MediaSpace, users can securely create, upload, share, search, browse, and watch live and on demand videos, presentations, screencasts, and other media content. But, this comes with a substantial price tag.

Oral history is almost always done for the purpose of sharing. Libraries, archives, and community groups can work together to share their work nearby and far away. Gathering the material and locking it away in an archives defeats the original intent. When you begin to plan the project, your stated mission will include ways to use and share the oral histories. The library or archives that will be the final home for the interviews will provide additional ways to share, both in the present and in the future. At all phases of the process it is important to think about how the material can be used in the future and how it will be accessible to community members and researchers in the easiest way possible.

Notes

1   Colorado State University-Pueblo, *Colorado Chicano/a Movement Archives*, Facebook page, Online, Available at HTTP: <www.facebook.com/coloradochicanomovement> (Accessed 3 January 2018).
2   For more information, see chapter 9 of Nancy MacKay's *Curating Oral Histories form Oral History to Archive*, 2nd ed. (New York: Routledge, 2016).
3   Society of American Archivists, *Website*, Online, Available at HTTP: <www2.archivists.org> (Accessed 3 January 2018). Also, see Appendix C for samples of finding aids.
4   ArchiveGrid, OCLC, *Website*, Available at HTTP: <www.oclc.org/research/themes/research-collections/archivegrid> (Accessed 3 January 2018).
5   "Terms of Service," YouTube, Online, Available at HTTP: <www.youtube.com/static?gl=CA&template=terms> (Accessed 3 January 2018).
6   See appendices for descriptions and links.
7   Digital Public Library of the United States, *Website*, Available at HTTP: <dp.la> (Accessed 3 January 2018).
8   Kaltura, *Website*, Available at HTTP: <corp.kaltura.com> (Accessed 3 January 2018).

8

ORAL HISTORY IN THE CLASSROOM

Classroom oral history projects are a fantastic way to build relationships between the university and the community and are a win-win situation for all parties involved. Not only do students have the opportunity to complete research in the surrounding community, and sometimes their own neighborhoods, but they also get practical experience building skills in recording technology, interviewing, and communications. This also gives the professor the opportunity to mentor students on research and scholarly presentations. And what elder could resist an opportunity to be interviewed by a young college student from his own neighborhood! An added advantage for the university archives is that the collections are expanded and more individuals become interested in research opportunities.

Realistically, oral history projects within the university structure are usually tied to an instructor who views collection as relevant to her students' class experience. Due to the structure of the university, and the fact that most funds are budgeted into permanent positions, it can be difficult to get outside resources, funding and staff for these types of projects. By collaborating with the university archivist or other departments on campus, instructors can gain access to recording equipment, transcription software, and can use the expertise of the archivist in storing and transferring information.

It should be noted that incorporating oral interviews can take considerable time away from a professor's research agenda. It may also be a venture that the professor's department may not value in regard to promotion and tenure. If it is of interest to a faculty member, but the faculty member has little or no experience, Don Ritchie's *Doing Oral History* (3rd ed.) lists oral history workshops for teachers and the Oral History Association website has a list of current workshops.[1] These can be in weeklong programs at a host site or they can be completed online.

Baylor University's "Workshops on the Web" is an excellent resource that can help keep the costs down.[2] Since these are at different times during the semester, you should contact the center to see what upcoming opportunities may be available. There is a cost associated with these types of workshops. However, they may be considered professional development opportunities by your administration. In regard to faculty involvement, it will save faculty members some time if their interest in oral history is tied into a class when they first get started. With the success of the class, faculty may think about how to add courses on oral history permanently into their department's curriculum and into their research agenda.

The Oral History Association is a great resource for faculty engaging on a new project as well as for a project that is already underway.[3] The Oral History Association website is a good place to go to find out more about resources in the classroom, grants, and publication opportunities. Instructors should look for articles about teaching in the *Oral History Review*.[4] These resources give a good perspective on the current state of oral history research, but also illustrate the varieties of projects that are being created with oral histories. If faculty members can combine what the students are doing in the classroom with their own research and publications, then projects like this will not detract too much from their own progress while in a tenure track position.

Collaborations

Don Ritchie suggests the possibility for oral history collaboration between universities and elementary schools.[5] Oral history interviews can be a learning tool in any discipline related to local history, community activism, media and technology, or history and archival research. Student projects can range from research and conducting interviews with community members, to audio and video documentary making, or to historical research using existing interviews from the archives. Community oral history has been successfully integrated into courses in ethnic studies, public history, immigration studies, urban studies, documentary making, and library and information science at the university level. Ritchie suggests that oral histories have been successful at institutions that have high minority enrollment and also at community colleges because oral history brings important historical moments, like the Civil Rights Movement, to life.[6] Oral histories also illustrate the importance of the individual in history. Oral interviews change how we see historical figures, rather than just looking at the lives of Presidents and leaders of movements.

Oral history allows teachers to facilitate a discovery of history. Rather than only seeing it in books, students have it come to life in front of them. For students, they are more attentive to what they are hearing from the narrator than they might be in a public presentation or if they were in a social situation. The interview can also bridge a generational gap between the interviewer and the narrator, since the interviewer may be in his late teens or early twenties while the narrator will most likely be over 60.[7]

Sample Assignments

Because of the versatility of majors and uses for oral histories, there is a wide variety of projects that could be assigned for students. In a journalism course, the oral interview could be used as the basis of an assignment highlighting the importance of accurate transcription. In a history course, oral histories could be used for a capstone paper. In mass communications classes, students could put together clips for social media or students could produce a documentary. The best assignments for the classroom are those that the professor sees as attached to the student's major and which can teach students hands-on practical application. The Houston Metropolitan Research Center at the Houston Public Library has partnered with the Spanish Department at the University of Houston-Downtown to have Spanish students transcribe oral interviews of individuals in the Houston community.[8] Students reflected on their experiences emphasizing that they did not understand how important their community was to the history of the nation.

At CSU-Pueblo, the Chicano/a Studies program has used oral interviews in upper division courses focused on the Chicano/a Movement and the Vietnam Conflict. These assignments have served two purposes: 1) giving students hands-on experience to learn about history in their home communities, and 2) finding new ways to think about giving oral presentations.

Here is a sample assignment for the course:

> *Oral History Projects*: One of the primary goals of this project (connecting the university with the community) is for students to take what they have learned in the classroom and apply it to their own community. Each student will conduct an oral interview with an individual in the community that is over the age of 70. (150 Pts)

This assignment allows the student to participate actively in the oral history process and create an archival-quality document that may be used by researchers. This will help students to feel invested in the project and its outcomes.

A writing component to the assignment will help students process their experience as well as keep a record of the tasks as they are accomplished. This will help them to understand the greater context of the interview and they can analyze how this may fit into the course topic and their field of study. A sample assignment may be:

> *Oral History Journal*: Each student will submit a 5–6 page journal of her/his experience with her/his oral interview. In the journal, students will show comparisons between their narrator and the leaders that we have discussed in the context of this course. (150 pts)

At Kennesaw State University in Georgia, Dr. Julia Brock, in her oral history course, has students complete active listening assignments.

> *Listening Exercises* (10%): During the first seven weeks of class, I'll give you an almost-weekly listening exercise that you will complete with a friend, family member, co-worker, or acquaintance. These exercises are meant to help you build your critical listening skills, an essential part of conducting oral histories. On Tuesdays, you will turn in a one-page response that reflects upon the questions in each listening exercise.[9]

Assignments like this give the students the opportunity to tune their listening and their conversations to be able to listen with a critical ear. These types of assignments also give the students an opportunity to practice their interviewing strategies ahead of time. By making the interviewer more comfortable, the narrator should also be more at ease.

At American University, Dr. Pamela M. Henson, in her Oral History Seminar Course, gives students a reflection assignment. Students interview a classmate for half an hour and then write a one to two page reflection of their experience during the interview. Students need to consider what they learned during the interview, especially any social interactions:

> What did you learn about the social interactions involved in an interview? Use specific examples to make your points, and pay special attention to nuances in tone, gesture, and expression, as well as language. If you were the one being interviewed, did the questions lead you in one direction and not another? Did you hold back information? Why? . . . Are there questions you wished you had asked? What are they? What lessons did you learn about doing oral history?[10]

An assignment like this is beneficial to the students because they have the opportunity to sit as the narrator. This can help the student learn what types of questions could make their informant uncomfortable and they may also learn why narrators may not be more talkative or open with their responses. These examples show the importance of having a class dedicated to oral interviews because students will be able to learn about the process before they complete the interview and it gives the students the time to develop a final project that they can link to their community.

At the University of Florida, Kathy Dwyer Navajas has incorporated oral histories into her Spanish 3948 Service Learning Course. Students interview Hispanic immigrants on a chosen theme and then complete a video oral history.

Using work as a focus of their research, the class divided into two person teams. Each team was required to develop, create, and edit a 5-minute "mini-doc" featuring a person selected and willing to tell his or her experiences and thoughts relating to work. The results were 11 compelling stories not only about work, but about the hard choices people face.[11]

Upon completion of the mini-doc, the projects were compiled into a larger documentary that was posted on Youtube and linked to the Samuel Proctor

Oral History Center webpage. This assignment is part of a larger initiative by the Samuel Proctor Oral History Center to collect oral histories related to the Latina/o Diaspora.[12]

Here is a sample assignment for a final project at CSU-Pueblo in a 400 level Chicano/a Studies course. This assignment shows the types of projects that students can present in the classroom. These can be easily adapted to be community presentations.

> *Final Presentation*: In groups of three to four, students will prepare a group project, either in the form of a 10 page paper, a 15–20 minute PowerPoint presentation, or a 10–15 minute video documentary. The project will address how Latinos' experiences during the Vietnam War connect to the rest of the course. The presentation should be grounded in historical fact, should clearly articulate the issue, and cite evidence for the argument. 150 points will be based on the presentation. The other 100 points will be based on your classmates' assessment of your contribution to the project. (250 points)

Whatever the final project, it should include a component of honoring the community documented, such as the community events mentioned above. Not only is this oral history best practice, but it is also a good way to build bridges, deepen understanding of other ways of life, make new friends and have a good time.

Showcasing Oral History Classroom work to the Community

For upper division or graduate level courses, a campus/community event could consist of a student presentation and honoring the narrators to highlight university/community relations; bringing both constituencies together for a fun and informative event. At CSU-Pueblo in the spring of 2011, the campus had the opportunity to host the traveling Vietnam Wall memorial. In the fall of 2009, students in an upper division course had completed 5–10 oral interviews with veterans of the Vietnam Conflict and the Korean War. Students completed short documentaries about these experiences. In the spring, in collaboration with the University Archives and the Chicano/a Studies program, narrators and students came together for a public presentation at the Wall to share the importance of the oral interview collection process. Students who were almost 40 years younger than the veterans expressed their heartfelt thanks for the veterans being willing to share the stories of their war experiences with them.

At Texas A&M Commerce, professors developed history courses that were specifically focused on oral history. The War and Memory course, which collects oral interviews, is also the training ground for oral historians to do internships in the University Archives. Students spend one semester taking a class which trains them in oral history and a second semester conducting interviews. This creates a pool of interviewers from which the Archives can recruit trained oral historians to serve as interns or work study students on a more long-term basis. Within the context of the course, students were able to identify their specific projects and if they moved on to the internship component, they had the ability to see those projects to fruition.[13] This has created a relationship between the students and the community that resulted in community members coming to the Archives with interest in the oral interview project rather than the archives having to reach out into the community.

Collaboration among departments on campus can stretch resources. It might be a good idea to work with the foreign language departments on campus to interview narrators who do not speak English. For example, students could perform the interviews in Spanish and translate them as a class assignment. There may be the opportunity to work with your university's alumni office to collect oral interviews of first generation alumni or alumni who have become prestigious in their fields. With proper direction, undergraduate students can make a valuable contribution towards helping create unique collections of primary sources while also earning course credit. Within the context of a one semester course, students can assist in the creation of an oral interview and have a project for a final presentation. This speeds up the oral interview processing and illustrates to the narrator that the project is completed quickly and efficiently.

Examples of Finished Projects

Oral History projects can be completed at both the undergraduate and graduate level. Teaching these courses at the graduate level may produce a more polished project. In 2004 and 2007, Dr. Karen Flint's graduate courses at the University of North Carolina-Charlotte collected oral histories of Brooklyn, New York. Interviews focused on the daily life of Brooklyn residents during the 1950s–1970s. Students contacted narrators, interviewed them, and transcribed interviews. The website <brooklyn-oral-history.uncc.edu> illustrates the type of finished project that can be created and illustrates how these audio interviews were shared.[14]

These types of projects are possible with a community that is interested in preserving its history and can create a space for non-traditional projects. Borderlands Theater in Tucson, Arizona has collaborated with Upward Bound, a grant funded program for low income and first generation college students to create an outdoor performance, *Barrio Stories*. *Barrio Stories* incorporated high school students into a university course, with students earning university and high school credit, in the collection and transcription of oral histories as well as in the performance of monologue pieces. The project's website[15] illustrates the process that Borderlands Theater used in the collection of the production including video clips and transcripts of interviews and images of the performance. This performance piece is an excellent example of how historians, community, and the university can collaborate to tell the story of their communities. Students were trained in playwriting and acting techniques to make their monologues more effective. For the students and the community that viewed the performance, this was a transformational piece because the students and the community saw their history come alive in theater.

When it comes to the classroom, there is a lot of potential for oral history projects. These can be one time projects or they can be websites or performance pieces. The most important things to remember are to create manageable projects, to understand the needs of the students, and to be respectful of the narrators. As you can see from *Barrio Stories*, these projects have the potential to live beyond the collection of the oral interview and to bring history alive in a non-traditional format. By making history come alive, the experience can be transformational for students and communities alike. For students, it can make history, which can be a dry subject, take on a living and immediate nature. It can give them more of a lens for looking at and understanding their own history as well as appreciating the history of the past.

Notes

1 Don Ritchie, *Doing Oral History* (New York: Oxford University Press, 3rd edition, 2014).
2 Baylor University Institute for Oral History, *Website*, HTTP: <www.baylor.edu/oralhistory> (Accessed 3 January 2018).
3 Oral History Association, *Website*, Available at HTTP: <www.oralhistory.org> (Accessed 3 January 2018).
4 Oxford University Press, *The Oral History Review*, Online, Available at HTTP: <academic.oup.com/ohr> (Accessed 3 January 2018).
5 Ritchie, *Doing Oral History*, 200–201.
6 Ibid, 216–217.
7 John Neuenschwander, *Oral history as a Teaching Approach* (Washington DC: National Education Association of the United States, 1976).
8 The Houston Metropolitan Research Center, *Website*, Available at HTTP: <www2.houstonlibrary.org/hmrc> (Accessed 3 January 2018).
9 Julia Brock, "HIST 4425: Oral History Syllabus," Online, Available at HTTP: <hp.hss.kennesaw.edu/syllabi/Fall14/HIST%204425%20Brock.pdf> (Accessed 3 January 2018).
10 Pamela M. Hensen, "Oral History Seminar," Online, Available at HTTP: <www.american.edu/cas/history/public/upload/Oral-History-2005-Henson.pdf> (Accessed 3 January 2018).
11 Samuel Proctor Oral History Center, *Website*, Available at HTTP: <oral.history.ufl.edu/projects/latinao-diaspora-in-the-americas-project/ldap-resources/spn-3948> (Accessed 3 January 2018).
12 Samuel Proctor Oral History Center, *Website*, HTTP: <oral.history.ufl.edu/projects/latinao-diaspora-in-the-americas-project> (Accessed 3 January 2018).
13 Andrea Weddle, 16 June 2015, interview with Beverly B. Allen and Fawn-Amber Montoya.
14 Brooklyn Oral History Project, *Website*, Available at HTTP: <brooklyn-oral-history.uncc.edu> (Accessed 3 January 2018).
15 Borderlands Theater and others, *Barrio Studies Project*, *Website*, Available at HTTP: <www.barriostories.org> (Accessed 3 January 2018).

9

PRESERVATION

This chapter will address the nuts and bolts of ensuring that oral history collections are preserved for future generations. But before getting into that, let's focus a little more about why we go to all this effort.

"What's past is prologue"

In William Shakespeare's play, *The Tempest*, Act II, scene i, Antonio declares that "what's past is prologue," attempting to convince Sebastian to murder his sleeping father in order to become king himself. In Antonio's mind, everything leading up to this event was simply a prologue to the great things to come.

The Merriam-Webster Dictionary defines 'prologue' as "an introductory or preceding event or development." A prologue "sets the scene" and provides some background information. As used by archivists and historians, this phrase is a warning not to forget the lessons of the past, because the past is a preface to the future.

The purpose of historical inquiry is the attempt to understand how people in the past thought and lived. In that context, consider the continually evolving nature of university/community relationships. Oral histories collected in one timeframe can inform the historians and scholars of a later age as they revisit and reinterpret a community's past. David B. Gracy III, speaking of historical records in a more general sense, believes that they:

> contribute to the continuity of culture by stimulating connections between the useful information from the past and the challenging needs of the present. They are records from a former present which contain vintage information, timely and exciting to the user who connects it to the present in which he or she labors.[1]

Making Decisions About Preservation

As with all other aspects of the oral history project, there needs to be a clear understanding and agreement between parties as to how the interviews will be preserved and accessed. Community partners may be more focused on short term goals like making the interviews available as soon as possible, and this may lead them to advocate for quick fixes, such as putting interviews up on YouTube, SoundCloud or some other commercial entity. They may not see the need for transcribing interviews, editing of video or audio recordings to add titles, etc., or what they may consider to be cumbersome paperwork. Community partners may want the interviews preserved, but they may not have the same concept of what long-term preservation requires as an archivist.

Institutions, on the other hand, generally take a longer-term view of preservation, and consider such platforms as YouTube and SoundCloud to be access portals only, not viable options for long-term preservation. They also consider the needs of future researchers, and ideally produce abstracts, indexes and/or transcriptions of interviews. Institutions are keenly aware of the inherent instability of internet commercial entities and realize the importance of redundancy. Will SoundCloud even be around next year? What will happen to the interviews uploaded there? Are they preserved elsewhere, or is SoundCloud or YouTube considered 'preservation.' Community members may become annoyed by delays caused by the university's focus on preserving the materials for posterity.

This makes the need for discussion and education as to best practices all the more important to avoid misunderstandings. A division of labor and responsibility should be spelled out in the Memorandum of Understanding, and time frames for deliverables established.[2]

Practical Considerations

Before a great collection of born-digital interviews has been created, it is necessary to ensure that they will be accessible in the long term. The choices made in terms of equipment, file formats and storage media will dramatically affect how accessible they will be in the future.

First of all, what do we mean by *digital preservation*? And how is it different from *backups*? While backups are a necessary first step, they do not constitute digital preservation. The Joint Information Systems (JISC), a United Kingdom-based scholarly communication initiative, notes these differences between back-up activities and a digital preservation program: "Disaster recovery strategies and backup systems are not sufficient to ensure survival and access to authentic digital resources over time. A backup is a short-term data recovery solution following loss or corruption and is fundamentally different to an electronic preservation archive."[3]

According to the ALCTS Preservation and Reformatting Section of the Working Group on Defining Digital Preservation,

TABLE 9.1 Version 1 of the Levels of Digital Preservation. Whatever level you are at with digital preservation, this table is a handy guide to ensure that you are covering all your bases.

	Level 1 (Protect your data)	Level 2 (Know your data)	Level 3 (Monitor your data)	Level 4 (Repair your data)
Storage and Geographic Location	• Two complete copies that are not collocated • For data on heterogeneous media (optical discs, hard drives, etc.) get the content off the medium and into your storage system	• At least three complete copies • At least one copy in a different geographic location • Document your storage system(s) and storage media and what you need to use them	• At least one copy in a geographic location with a different disaster threat • At least three copies in geographic locations with different disaster threats • Obsolescence monitoring process for your storage system(s) and media	• Have a comprehensive plan in place that will keep files and metadata on currently accessible media or systems
File Fixity and Data Integrity	• Check file fixity on ingest if it has been provided with the content • Create fixity info if it wasn't provided with the content	• Check fixity on all ingests • Use write-blockers when working with original media • Virus-check high risk content	• Check fixity of content at fixed intervals • Maintain logs of fixity info; supply audit on demand • Ability to detect corrupt data • Virus-check all content	• Check fixity of all content in response to specific events or activities • Ability to replace/repair corrupted data • Ensure no one person has write access to all copies

Information Security	• Identify who has read, write, move and delete authorization to individual files • Restrict who has those authorizations to individual files	• Document access restrictions for content	• Maintain logs of who performed what actions on files, including deletions and preservation actions	• Perform audit of logs
Metadata	• Inventory of content and its storage location • Ensure backup and non-collocation of inventory	• Store administrative metadata • Store transformative metadata and log events	• Store standard technical and descriptive metadata	• Store standard preservation metadata
File Formats	• When you can give input into the creation of digital files encourage use of a limited set of known open formats and codecs	• Inventory of file formats in use	• Monitor file format obsolescence issues	• Perform format migrations, emulation and similar activities as needed

Credit: National Digital Stewardship Alliance

Digital preservation combines policies, strategies and actions to ensure access to reformatted and born digital content regardless of the challenges of media failure and technological change. The goal of digital preservation is the accurate rendering of authenticated content over time.

Digital preservation strategies and actions address content creation, integrity and maintenance.

Content creation includes: clear and complete technical specifications; production of reliable master files; sufficient descriptive, administrative and structural metadata to ensure future access; and detailed quality control of processes.

Content integrity includes: documentation of all policies, strategies and procedures; use of persistent identifiers; recorded provenance and change history for all objects; verification mechanisms; attention to security requirements; and routine audits.

Content maintenance includes: a robust computing and networking infrastructure; storage and synchronization of files at multiple sites; continuous monitoring and management of files; programs for refreshing, migration and emulation; creation and testing of disaster prevention and recovery plans; and periodic review and updating of policies and procedures.[4]

According to Leigh Grinstead, Digital Services Consultant at Lyrasis:

best practice recommends a high level of redundancy—at least three copies, on two different media, kept at geographically dispersed locations. As we learned with hurricane Katrina, across campus may not be enough! Look at backing up in different states, regions, or using cloud-based backup systems to gain the geographic diversity necessary.[5]

To learn more about evaluating cloud-based options see Seth Anderson's "Feet on the Ground: A Practical Approach to the Cloud: Nine Things to Consider When Assessing Cloud Storage."[6]

Another helpful resource is the "Levels of Digital Preservation" currently being finalized by the National Digital Stewardship Alliance (NDSA). "Levels of Digital Preservation" is a work in progress which sets out a tiered set of recommendations on how organizations should begin to build or enhance their digital preservation activities. The work is intended to be a relatively easy-to-use set of guidelines useful not only for those just beginning to think about preserving their digital assets, but also for institutions planning the next steps in enhancing their existing digital preservation systems and workflows.[7]

Formats

We are in a time of rapidly changing technologies, so best practices for the long-term preservation of digital oral histories are somewhat in flux. As a general rule, however, when creating digital files in the interview process, consider the following criteria:

- The preservation master file should ideally be in an uncompressed lossless format. When *lossless* formats are used, there is no loss of data from the original file. On the other hand, when files are saved in *lossy* formats, the data are compressed, which results in smaller files, but loss of data. This means that they will deteriorate more quickly over time than uncompressed, *lossless* files.[8]
- Uncompressed files, especially video, can be *very* large, so when planning for the project, ensure that there is enough hard drive and/or network space to accommodate them. You may decide, based on the size of the files, to pilot a project of 10–15 oral histories to understand potential file sizes. You can also use a file size calculator to estimate the storage space needed for your project.[9,10] For example, one hour of audio gathered at a sample rate of 44.1(Hz) and 16-bit depth will generate a file that is 620.2 MB. On the other hand, one hour of NTSC uncompressed 10-bit video can run up to 105.5 GB.

Digital storage over the long haul can be expensive but the loss of irreplaceable content is unmeasurable. In addition to the uncompressed master files, smaller compressed files are created known as, mezzanine copies or service masters that can be used to create the necessary files for researcher and online use. Smaller files are appropriate for access purposes, will load faster, and take up less space on the website, digital repository or other hosting service.

Master files need to have checksums generated upon capture and be backed up to a remote location to ensure that if the local server should be struck by disaster, that the files can be restored. According to the Digital Preservation Handbook, "a checksum on a file is a 'digital fingerprint' whereby even the smallest change to the file will cause the checksum to change completely."[11]

Further, non-proprietary formats are preferred for the preservation of master files. Choose a widely used open source format to avoid compatibility issues down the road and so that files can be more easily migrated later.

The U.S. National Archives currently has these recommendations for the digital audio and video files that it will accept and they can serve as guidelines for both the creation and preservation of master files.

- *Video:* Audio-Video Interleave format (AVI), QuickTime format (MOV), Material Exchange Format (MXF)
- *Audio:* Audio Interchange File Format (AIFF), Uncompressed Waveform audio format (WAV), Audio format (AU), Uncompressed Broadcast Wave Format (BWF), Free format Lossless Audio Codec (FLAC), Audio Lossless Coding format (ALS).[12]

A variety of factors can play into the decisions associated with this issue and the literature on the subject can be overwhelming and technically confusing. But one rule of thumb to remember is this: the perfect is the enemy of the good. Make the best choices possible based on your budget, local infrastructure and available expertise.

Software for Oral History

Various types of software exist for video and audio editing, and for transcription:

Video Editing Software

- *Adobe Premiere Pro (PC)*—timeline-based software that supports high resolution video editing and is part of Adobe Creative Cloud, which includes video editing, graphic design, and web development programs.
- *Final Cut Pro (Mac)*—non-linear video editing software program for Quick-Time and compatible formats
- *iMovie (Mac)*—video editing software application for the Mac and iOS (iPhone, iPad, iPad Mini and iPod Touch)[13]

Audio Recording/Editing Software

- *Audacity*—free open source digital audio editor and recording computer software application, available for Windows, OS X, Linux and other operating systems.
- *Adobe Audition*—PC or Mac, part of Adobe Creative Cloud
- *Sound Forge*—digital audio software aimed at pro and semi-pro market[14]

Transcribing Software

The process of transcribing interviews is not as widespread as it once was. Transcription is a time-consuming and detail oriented pursuit, open to some interpretation by the transcriber. Even if the transcription of interviews is a future goal, it may be desirable to upload video and audio content to the internet as a means of making the materials widely available quickly. If the decision is made to transcribe interviews, there are several transcription software packages available which are inexpensive and easy to use. While still labor intensive, these programs can speed up the time involved in transcribing an interview.

- *InqScribe*—It works with both audio and video, allows insertion of time codes and to easily share transcripts with others.
- *Google Transcribe*—Add-on for Google Chrome browser, keyboard shortcuts—to pause, slow-down, speed-up, rewind or fast-forward the audio clip, can be used online or offline; auto-saves transcribed text.
- *Express Scribe*—features variable speed playback, multi-channel control, playing video, file management.[15]

- *Popup Archive*—a potentially useful product which claims to tag, index and create transcripts automatically. If you have a great many interviews to process, it may be worth investigating.[16]

Metadata

Metadata, or 'data about data', will also need to be created for the interviews. Descriptive metadata consists of a description of the contents, creator, date created, copyright information, permissions, licenses and intellectual property rights.

In order to provide long-term access to any digital files, such as oral histories, however, there is a need to capture significantly more than just descriptive metadata. Administrative metadata such as provenance, custodial history, rights to use and access, as well any preservation and technical metadata such as file size, authenticity and format should also be captured while processing. Structural metadata including how the files are organized and how the parts relate to the whole should be tracked as well.

A potentially useful software product is Oral History Metadata Synchronizer (OHMS). This is a free, open source, web-based system which works with the content management system to (enhance access to oral history files online. While OHMS does not create transcripts or indexes, it provides users with the ability to create and tie tags to specific text in audio/video or to a transcript or index.[17]

There are currently no widely agreed upon standards for oral history metadata, however collaborating with metadata librarians may help. Also, Elinor Maze shares advice on the Oral History Association website in her article, "Metadata: Best practices for oral history access and preservation."[18]

Conclusion: Redundancy, Redundancy!

Digital preservation is a complicated issue, but it is worth emphasizing yet again that the first step for ensuring the survival of your digital files is redundancy, and storage in geographically diverse locations! Digital files are inherently fragile and without proper upkeep and maintenance access may not be possible. Digital files do degrade and computers do crash, so monitoring, and a strategy for migration will be critical over the long term.

Maintain as many copies as possible in different locations, on site and off site. Institutions do this in a variety of ways. Some, like the Oregon State Multicultural Archives, rely on a RAID array in house with cloud backup.[19] Others, like CSU-Pueblo, maintain a RAID array in house and backup to a dedicated network server in a different location. Some institutions rely on their institutional repositories to serve as a backup to their in-house files. Other institutions may decide to use an outside vendor to manage their digital files; this obviates the need to develop a costly infrastructure and significant in house expertise. According to Adam C. Northem, Digital Collections Librarian at Texas A&M-Commerce:

our digital master files, specifically those that are used to make derivatives that go into our digital collections, are stored and managed by OCLC's Digital Archive service. We send our archival digital files to a Cloud server, and they store them, back them up, and create checksums and perform fixity checks for us. It is very convenient, because storage of digital files has always been one of our biggest concerns. It is a bit inconvenient if we need to retrieve any of those files, however. Many of them are large video files, and they are not able to be uploaded/downloaded via network due to bandwidth limitations. We keep access copies of those files stored on campus so they can be used in most cases, but if necessary, we could have our master files shipped back to us on a hard drive.[20]

Still others with more limited budgets may store their files on a hard drive with CD backups in a different geographical location. Similarly, you may not be able to commit to the continuing expense of vendor management or cloud storage; it is often easier to justify a one-time expense for a RAID array. It is absolutely essential, however, to ensure that there is at least one backup of the files in a separate location, so that if disaster strikes, the files can be restored.

While some digital solutions are better than others, there is not necessarily one 'right' way. The solution you choose will depend on your budget, your level of expertise, and the resources you can muster.

Just like the interview process, ensuring the preservation of the interviews you have so laboriously collected requires pre-planning and planning for the future at all phases of the project. Investing in digital preservation requires a serious commitment on the part of an institution and should not be taken lightly. It is not just an investment on the part of the oral history archives, library or program, but also the university's Information Management, IT or Systems department. Administrative buy-in is also essential. Digital preservation, however, is essential if these valuable resources are to be available to inform later generations of scholars, students and the general public.

Notes

1 David B. Gracy III, "Is there a Future in the Use of Archives," *Archivaria* (Summer 1987): 24: 9.
2 See Chapter 4 for discussion of Memorandums of Understanding.
3 JISC. *Digital Preservation: Continued Access to Authentic Digital Assets*, briefing paper (2006): 5, Online, Available at HTTP: <www.webarchive.org.uk/wayback/archive/20140615231719/http://www.jisc.ac.uk/media/documents/publications/digitalpreservationbp.pdf> (Accessed 3 January 2018).
4 ALCTS, *Definitions of Digital Preservation*, 2007, Online, Available at HTTP: <www.ala.org/alcts/resources/preserv/defdigpres0408> (Accessed 3 January 2018).
5 Katherine Skinner and Matt Schultz, eds., "A Guide to Distributed Digital Preservation," Online, Available at HTTP: <open.bu.edu/bitstream/handle/2144/1351/GDDP_Educopia.pdf?sequence=1> (Accessed 16 January 2018).
6 Seth Anderson, "Feet on the Ground: A Practical Approach to the Cloud. Nine Things to Consider When Assessing Cloud Storage," *AV Preserve* (2014), Online, Available at

HTTP: <www.avpreserve.com/wp-content/uploads/2014/02/AssessingCloudStorage. pdf > (Accessed 3 January 2018).

7 NSDA, *Levels of Digital Preservation*, Online, Available at HTTP: <ndsa.org/activities/ levels-of-digital-preservation> (Accessed 3 January 2018).

8 Barbara Goldsmith, "Digitizing Video for Long-Term Preservation: An RFP Guide and Template," 2013, Online, Available at HTTP: <memoriav.ch/wp-content/uploads/ 2014/07/VARRFP.pdf> (Accessed 3 January 2018).

9 Digital Rebellion, *Video Space Calculator*, Online, Available at HTTP: <www.digital rebellion.com/webapps/videocalc> (Accessed 3 January 2018).

10 The Audio Archive, *Audio File Size Calculator*, Online, HTTP: <www.theaudioarchive. com/TAA_Resources_File_Size.htm> (accessed 3 January 2018).

11 Digital Preservation Coalition, *Digital Preservation Handbook*, Online, Available at HTTP: <www.dpconline.org/handbook/technical-solutions-and-tools/fixity-and-checksums> (Accessed 3 January 2018).

12 National Archives, *Appendix A: Tables of File Formats*, Online, Available at HTTP: <www.archives.gov/records-mgmt/policy/transfer-guidance-tables.html> (Accessed 3 January 2018).

13 See appendices for further information and links to these products.

14 See appendices for further information and links to these products.

15 See appendices for further information and links to these products.

16 Popup Archive, *Website*, Available at HTTP: <www.popuparchive.com> (Accessed 3 January 2018).

17 Oral History Online, *Oral History Metadata Synchronizer*, Online, Available at HTTP: <www.oralhistoryonline.org> (Accessed 3 January 2018).

18 Elinor A. Mazé, "Metadata: Best Practices for Oral History Access and Preservation", Online, Available at HTTP: <ohda.matrix.msu.edu/2012/06/metadata> (Accessed 3 January 2018).

19 RAID provides a way of storing the same data in different places (thus, redundantly) on multiple hard disks.

20 Email, 8 December 2017, Adam C. Northem, to Beverly B. Allen.

10

COMMUNITY COLLABORATIONS

Fawn-Amber Montoya

As a history professor and advisor for undergraduate history majors, I am constantly looking for opportunities to offer hands-on experiences in history for my students. Hands-on experiences allow them to consider history as a possible profession, and also allows them to get excited about their major. I live in the community that I studied in graduate school. It is also the home of my ancestors. For me, history is both personally and professionally satisfying. I try to bring excitement about the region into my courses and I have the opportunity to focus on the ethnic heritage of the region. Occasionally, I come across a student from southern Colorado who has an interest in history. José Antonio Ortega is one of these students. José's work has given him the opportunity to link his personal and professional life.

José's motivation and love of his community brought him to study history at CSU-Pueblo. He was able to secure a research position from the Provost's office and from that he pursued his vision for how to connect his family history and experiences to academic research.

José Antonio Ortega

Growing up on the east side of Pueblo, Colorado, the University of Southern Colorado (currently known as CSU-Pueblo) always seemed like it was a world away, even though it was less than two miles from where I grew up. I only knew about the football team, the annual Fourth of July celebration and the rare Cinco de Mayo events that my aunt attended as a student and I occasionally tagged along. When I enrolled in CSU-Pueblo in 2011, I was initially a psychology major. I quickly found that many of my professors either came from a different demographic from myself or were from out of town. While attending my Introduction to Chicano/a Studies course, I found that the material made sense to me and I could see myself reflected in the history. On a number of occasions, I spoke to Dr. Montoya about this and we discussed possible careers in which I could use my love of history and my desire to tell the story of my community.

I switched my major to history and got the opportunity to work in the Archives and Special Collections at the university. I had a lot of people pulling for me to gain the position. I grew up within a circle of people who were highly active in the Chicano/a Movement in Denver and Pueblo. My *tío*, José Esteban Ortega, and my father, José Anselmo Ortega, were at CU-Boulder in the early 1970s when there were rallies, sit-ins, protests and administrative building takeovers. My *tío* was a leader and an organizer for many of these events. Juan Federico Trujillo, AKA 'Freddie Freak,' the self-proclaimed unofficial archivist of the Colorado Chicano/a Movement, who was also in attendance at the University of Colorado, Boulder, is a close friend of mine. It was a natural fit for me to work on the Chicano/a Movement collections because of my associations with the people and the community. These associations made it easier for me to process collections, transcribe oral histories, and identify pictures and videos. Students without these associations may be able to process the collection but will not be able to identify people, places or events.

Throughout my years as a history major I learned much about Colorado, the United States and the world. I had some great professors here at CSU-Pueblo but most of them did not have any knowledge of my community's culture. Sure, they may have known about the Mexican food around Pueblo and maybe even heard about how you should not venture into the east side after dark. They knew relatively nothing about the people and their struggle for equal rights. These types of disconnects currently continue and can make it difficult for students who do not understand the value of community stories within history.

In the summer of 2014, I was awarded a grant called a Summer Undergraduate Research Project through the Office of the Provost at CSU-Pueblo. The focus of this research project was the Salt Creek community in Pueblo, Colorado, and Louie "Lugs" Garcia's community activism in the 1970s.[1] Salt Creek is located to the west of the Colorado Fuel and Iron Company (now Evraz Rocky Mountain Steel), one of the largest steel mills west of the Mississippi river in the 1900s. The Colorado Fuel and Iron method of smelting slag was later found to be forming a hazardous byproduct for the environment. The slag was dumped into the water which the lower section of the Salt Creek community relied on for drinking, cooking, and bathing. The health of the residents in the lower section of Salt Creek began to decline. The older residents in the community needed someone to stand up and fight in order to be hooked up to the water from the St. Charles Mesa Water Sanitation District.

There were many obstacles facing Louie and his supporters. One of the main obstacles was the division in the Salt Creek community. The upper and lower sections were divided because most of the people in the upper section already had clean water. Their land was platted in uniform sections, and the residents were more economically stable and were tied to the county commissioners. The lower section's land was not platted uniformly. It had natural borders in conjunction with the landscape. The lower section was overrun with trash, debris, and abandoned homes, and did not have access to clean water. The division within the small community caused many differing versions of the events that took place.

Many people in Salt Creek have different versions, ideas or simply do not remember the things that were going on in this little community. My mother, Lorraine Nunez, grew up on San Juan Street which borders the upper section and lower section. When I began my research, she was the first person I had asked about the goings on and what she remembered. She could tell me a lot of things that were happening in the upper section. She was not very helpful when it came to the lower section. After more research was gathered about Louie "Lugs"—the protests, marches, rallies and cleanup—I thought that I'd check back to see if maybe any of this new information might spark memories from my mother. She would say things like, "I don't remember that happening" and "I don't remember seeing or hearing that." I joked with her and told her, "See, you were part of the problem." She said these things as if I were making them up. There was such a disconnect within this small community that my mother, who was in her mid-teens, did not know the struggles of people who were on the other side of the hill.

Other versions of what took place in Salt Creek have become much of the dialogue, and this history of environmental contamination has been lost from the history that is told in the community today. Louie "Lugs" passed away and did not have an oral history but he did keep handwritten notes in several notebooks. While I was working in the Archives, we received a new Chicano/a Movement collection which had a video. I was asked to view it because it had several clips of rallies, protests, interviews, and performances which were mainly held in Pueblo. As I sifted through the video I came across a short interview with Louie and his wife, Delfina. The interview was held in Salt Creek and he talked about the lack of representation for the community in the Pueblo City Council meetings. He also talked about how the City Council was trying to buy the land owned by the residents of Salt Creek at the original cost and not at an appreciated value. Although the video clip was short, Louie touched on hotly debated issues.

Delfina and her daughter Gloria Ramirez corroborated Louie's story in their oral histories. When I started the research on my project it was by pure chance that they visited Pueblo at the same time. They both suffer from health-related issues and traveling is extremely hard for them. My sister Matrina and my mother were visiting with Delfina and Gloria. They started talking about how their husband/father fought for clean water. They wanted to visit the CSU-Pueblo Archives so that they could look through the Garcia collection. We thought this was an opportune time to conduct an interview. I interviewed Delfina and Gloria at the same time. They shared stories about the fight in Salt Creek. They named important people in the fight and in the opposition. Their oral history was a great complement to my research.

After I had completed my research, I began construction on a Prezi presentation.[2] My first presentation was to be held at CSU-Pueblo. I immediately thought about my audience when I started creating my Prezi. I decided it would be important to show exactly where Salt Creek was in relation to the university because I knew many of the people, such as professors, administrators, and students, who would attend but would not know where Salt Creek is located. So, I chose to use a map of Salt Creek as the background and I had many of my slides pop up from different places in the community. The map was also used to show how close CF&I was to Salt Creek. I added several slides, photos and the interview with Louie. On the night of the presentation, all 100 seats in the auditorium were taken and there was only standing room in the back. I was shocked that so many people attended the presentation, but for the first time I really came to realize how important the work that I was doing was to me and to my community.

My second presentation was held at the Fulton Heights Recreation Hall in Salt Creek. Dr. Montoya and I knew that the issues in Salt Creek were still sensitive because of the opposing sides. In the community, there are a number of people who lay claim to all the improvements in Salt Creek. We knew that people from the opposing sides would come to the presentation and that there might be some tension. After completing the presentation, I started the Q&A with the audience. At first, a gentleman began to question my research. He questioned my age—I am in my late 30s—and insinuated that I was too young to research or remember the events in Salt Creek. Another elderly gentleman rose up and began to ask questions. The man from the back raised his voice and said, "If there's anything you need to know about Salt Creek, that's who you ask—that man right there." He pointed and the man stood up.

The man he was referring to was, as I later found out, his father. This man was a representative from the community. He got up and began to talk about all of his accomplishments in Salt Creek. He asked me, "Do you know who got the water for this block?" He pointed to himself. He said, "Do you know who got the streetlights for this block?" He, again, pointed to himself. During the Q&A, it was the opponents of Louie "Lugs" who took credit for the community's accomplishments. The tension in the room was heightened because some of Louie's children were in the audience. One sister exclaimed, "You weren't the only one to do something for this community!" The gentleman just continued to speak about his own accomplishments and brushed aside the comment. He was a power player in the community and had powerful friends to match. Beverly Allen, the archivist, and I approached him about conducting an oral history with him. He left the possibility open but turned us down because he could not foresee when he would be available as he was preparing the budget for the community.

It was important to be in the community of Salt Creek and conduct the presentation. After the event CSU-Pueblo Archives and Special Collections and El Pueblo History Museum collaborated on a memory workshop for Salt Creek residents. We used my presentation to get people out and motivated to tell their stories. Advertisements were sent out and our local newspaper, the *Pueblo Chieftain*, published an article. I offered rides to people who did not have a means to get there on their own. We held the workshop the following weekend after my presentation because we felt that it would still be on their minds and the motivation would be high.

The memory workshop was held at the El Pueblo Museum on Saturday, November 8th, 2014. Unbeknown to all of us, there was a parade scheduled for Veteran's Day. There were roadblocks all around the museum. After speaking to the police, they allowed one entrance to the parking lot. We were discouraged because we thought that it might prevent people from attending the workshop. To our surprise people began to arrive. The tables began to fill up quickly. Over 40 people attended the workshop. The museum director, Dawn DiPrince, conducted the workshop. She started the workshop off by having the attendees draw a picture of the floor plan of their homes. She then had them focus on rooms and try to remember what they saw, heard and smelled. After completing the picture portion of the workshop, she told everyone to write about what they remembered. People stood up and read their stories to everyone. Some people were apprehensive about sharing what they wrote. After a few people read their stories more and more people began to share. It quickly turned from people sharing their individual stories to people telling a collaborative story. The room became loud with memories and laughter. Although the division between the upper and lower residents is still an underlying issue in Salt Creek, the people came together that day and even razzed each other about the differences between them.

Another attempt was made to hold a memory workshop at El Pueblo Museum. Not one resident from Salt Creek showed up to this event. The word did not spread through the community as well as the first workshop. Plus, we did not have an event like my presentation to get the people motivated.

Having a student such as myself, who is from the very same community, gathering oral histories makes the conversation flow easier. Relating to people on a personal level makes them more comfortable and increases the likelihood that they may divulge more information than they would otherwise tell an outsider.

Instead of just listening to Delfina and Gloria tell me a story of their past, I became an active participant in the conversation. I was able to clarify some of their statements because I knew some of the people, places, and events in and around Salt Creek. It was also helpful that I spent a lot of time in walking around Salt Creek growing up. The geography of this little community can easily make a person travel in circles and knowing the little nooks and crannies that they spoke of made it easier for them to explain where certain events happened.

The university can attract more students from the community by offering more classes that focus specifically on Pueblo and the surrounding region. Pueblo has a rich history that was not taught in Colorado history courses that I previously enrolled in. The book that was assigned had small pieces of local history, such as industrialist William Jackson Palmer, the railroad and the Colorado Fuel and Iron Co. However, teaching classes that tell the stories of Denver and Colorado Springs cannot be indicative to the story of Pueblo. Teaching only big city history leaves out Pueblo's contributions and the people who make up the community.

What Is a Memory Workshop

Memory Workshop – A memory workshop is a community gathering in which individuals share in discussion about their experiences. These workshops should be held in places that are seen as community gathering spaces and spaces that are accessible, parking and physically, to attendees. Once attendees have arrived,

1. Have all attendees introduce themselves.
2. Have them write about a memory that they have of an event which you are hoping to document.
3. Have each individual share their experience if they are willing to.

Since attendance at these events can range from a handful of people to an audience of 50. It is important to think about those who want to share their stories to have time allotted. Ideally, you would set aside time on a Saturday for 2–3 hours. If these are recorded, be sure to get permission from attendees to record. If there is not enough time for all attendees to share, invite them back for follow up interviews. For those who share their memories, this is a good opportunity to decide who you may want to have a follow up interview with.

FIGURE 10.1 Memory workshops can be a useful tool to jog narrators' memories

Also, teaching students from outside of Pueblo can be beneficial because they can feel connected to the city in which they attend college.

Offering a class on Pueblo's history can also serve another purpose towards documentation of the region through oral history. If the school does not have a student that they can rely on to take these types of community based oral histories, then they can either bring in an interviewer from the community or teach classes on how to conduct oral histories. Giving the potential interviewers a base knowledge of the community would help immensely because they become part of the narrator's conversation instead of an interviewer reading a prepared set of questions.

After the great response we received after the presentation, it is clear that more funding should be given to student projects. Having more and more students conduct projects like mine on different communities, people, ethnicities and events in and around Pueblo could gain more respect for the university. It would show that the university has an interest in the surrounding town. The more oral histories that are gathered from the community, the more of a voice is given to the people who would otherwise be silent. It makes the university more accessible to the community through presentations and collections of archives.

Fawn-Amber Montoya

José's work in the Archives and his future goals have helped us to think in more depth about the collaborations between students and the community and between faculty and the community. Oral history projects not only have the potential to shape curriculum for students, but to also serve as evidence of the university's strategic mission. By collaborating with offices on campus and thinking about the student's experience within the university setting, you will find advocates who envision their future in archives and in libraries, but who also see the community as central to their academic experience.

Notes

1 Fawn-Amber Montoya, "Salt Creek Memory Project," Online, Available at HTTP: <www.youtube.com/watch?v=04zMYj1AI0k> (Accessed 3 January 2018).
2 José A. Ortega, "Barrio de Salado. Community Unification and Improvement." Online, Available at HTTP: <prezi.com/wnekugcdp13c/salt-creek> (Accessed 3 January 2018).

CONCLUSION

Now that we have reached the end, we hope that we have given you a strong understanding of the benefits of a community/university relationship in documenting local history through oral interviews with community members. Oral history projects that grow out of such relationships are complicated and come with inherent challenges as we have discussed.

While these types of projects can take a lot of time and negotiation, they are rewarding for the university and for the community. Most importantly it helps to preserve the stories of community members while providing valuable learning opportunities for students. This is also a process; you will not necessarily get it right the first time and as with any project there will be discussions and a reframing of the project at multiple points.

In its role as a research institution, it is important for the university partner to have a rigorous plan for creation, preservation, and use of the interviews. This is why many oral history programs, such as the one at CSU-Pueblo, are administered within the library or archives. Current archives best practices emphasize a proactive approach to publicizing collections—to both the scholarly community and the local community. Ideally students, faculty, and administrators will understand that the interview projects are worthwhile scholarly sources for academic research.

The relationship between the community and the university is multi-faceted and what works in one part of the university may not represent what is happening overall in the relationship. The oral interview process, even if within the context of a few years, creates a more tangible and collaborative space for the university and the community to engage with each other. This type of project can give students hands on experience in oral history techniques, experiential education in their courses, and a great connection to the community in which their institution is located.

A Faculty Perspective: Fawn-Amber Montoya

From a faculty perspective, oral history collection is an invaluable source of research material. I have used oral interviews that were collected in the 1970s and the 1980s focused on events that occurred in the 1910s. I will always be grateful to oral historians who recorded these interviews because they have helped me to expand my research. There is also something powerful about hearing a person describe a historical event in her own words. This brings a new relationship with the research subject or with the historical event.

As a teacher, I have found the oral history interview to be a great way to connect students to their community and to the past. When students have participated in oral history collection they have commented afterwards that they did not realize how much history was in their community.

These community oral history projects have helped me to build stronger connections with the community that has made me feel more at home and helped me to realize that relationships with the community not only help me to better frame my research but also to understand the impact of the individual on historical events.

An Archivist's Perspective: Beverly B. Allen

I have not always been a big fan of doing oral history, especially after my experience with it in my early career, when the project, due to poor planning, became unwieldy and overwhelming. It was a long time before I was willing to give it another go.

However, eight years ago, I came to work at CSU-Pueblo and became the person responsible for building the ethnic heritage and diversity archives. In some ways, this job has been a different experience from previous ones, in the sense that it was the first time that I have been working primarily with living donors, that is to say, donors who are also the creators of the materials they are giving us, rather than their descendants. This is a very different dynamic from working in an archives where the donor of the records is more removed from them, sometimes by several generations. Because my donor-creators are so close to the records, they generally have a much stronger desire to be part of the process for making decisions relating to those records. As the curator for archival collections of people who have been dead for many years, one gets used to having the freedom to make one's own decisions about the collections. In many ways, it's much easier. However, as I've learned since coming to CSU-Pueblo, that's not necessarily the best way to work. I remember going to professional meetings and hearing colleagues talk about how making decisions about what records to keep was sort of like 'playing God', since by those decisions, we were influencing the historical record, deciding what parts of history were important and which were not.

Should one person have the power to make those kinds of decisions? I don't think so. History doesn't 'belong' to any one person—it belongs to us all, and we can have different opinions of what's significant. My experience here has given me so much more insight into what the creators of the records, for example, think is important. I've grown to embrace the role of 'steward' rather than 'owner', accepting a collaborative role, and not thinking that because I'm the records 'professional' that my opinion is always the best or most representative of the historical record.

I also think some in our profession have been dubious about the value of oral history and denigrated it as 'too subjective.' What such critics often fail to realize, however, is that letters, diaries and other 'written' records can be every bit as 'subjective' as oral testimonies. The role of the historian and the student is to critically evaluate the historical evidence before him, not to take it at face value. In that sense, oral histories have every bit as much credibility as the more tangible documents.

As archivists and historians, we are frequently frustrated by the gaps we find in archival sources. For me, oral history has been an important way to help fill in some of those gaps in the historical record. Oral history is also an important tool to help gather evidence about the history of underrepresented groups, which in some cases, tend to have more of an oral than a written tradition. Capturing these oral testimonies may be the best way to document some cultures.

Doing oral history also has the benefit of getting archivists out of the archives and into the community, which can only make our work more understandable and relevant to the communities we serve. Academics are notorious for not wanting to leave our ivory towers to venture out into the 'real' world. Collaborations such as oral history projects provide an important way for the gown to connect with the town. These partnerships can work to the benefit of both, promoting greater understanding and effectiveness. In short, they create a common ground for future cooperative efforts between university and community.

APPENDIX A

Works Cited

ALCTS. *Definitions of Digital Preservation*. Online. Available at HTTP: <www.ala.org/alcts/resources/preserv/defdigpres0408> (Accessed 3 January 2018).

Anderson, Seth. "Feet on the Ground: A Practical Approach to the Cloud. Nine Things to Consider When Assessing Cloud Storage." *AV Preserve*. 2014. Online. Available at HTTP: <www.avpreserve.com/wp-content/uploads/2014/02/AssessingCloudStorage.pdf> (Accessed 3 January 2018).

ArchivesNext. *Links from MAC Talk on Participatory Archives*. Online. Available at HTTP: <www.archivesnext.com/?p=2716> (Accessed 3 January 2018).

Audio Archive, The. *Audio File Size Calculator*. Online. Available at HTTP: <www.theaudioarchive.com/TAA_Resources_File_Size.htm> (Accessed 3 January 2018).

Baxley, Austin and Eric L. Gruver. "Creating an Integrated School: A Divergent Perspective from East Texas." *Sound Historian* 16 (2014): 19–30.

Baylor University Institute for Oral History. *Online Workshops*. Online. Available at HTTP: <www.baylor.edu/oralhistory/index.php?id=931747> (Accessed 3 January 2018).

Baylor University Institute for Oral History. *Website*. Available at HTTP: <www.baylor.edu/oralhistory/> (Accessed 3 January 2018).

Borderlands Theater and others. *Barrio Studies Project*. Online. Available at HTTP: <www.barriostories.org/> (Accessed 3 January 2018).

Boyd, Doug. "Audio or Video for Recording Oral History: Questions, Decisions." Online. Available at HTTP: <ohda.matrix.msu.edu/2012/06/audio-or-video-for-recording-oral-history/> (Accessed 3 January 2018).

Brock, Julia. "HIST 4425: Oral History Syllabus." Online. Available at HTTP: <hp.hss.kennesaw.edu/syllabi/Fall14/HIST%204425%20Brock.pdf> (Accessed 3 January 2018).

Brown, Aimee. "How Queer 'Packrats' and Activist Archivists Saved our History: An Overview of Lesbian, Gay, Bisexual, Transgender, and Queer (LGBTQ) Archives, 1970–2008." In *Serving LGBTIQ Library and Archives Users: Essays on Outreach, Service, Collections and Access*. (Ed.) Ellen Greenblatt. Jefferson, NC: McFarland & Company.

Collegefactual,com. *How Diverse is Texas A&M-Commerce?* Online. Available at HTTP: <www.collegefactual.com/colleges/texas-a-and-m-university-commerce/student-life/diversity/> (Accessed 3 January 2018).

Colorado Historic Newspaper Collection. *La Cucaracha*. Online. Available at HTTP: <www.coloradohistoricnewspapers.org/cgi-bin/colorado?a=cl&cl=CL1&sp=LCP&e=------en-20--1--txt-txIN--------0-> (Accessed 3 January 2018).

Colorado State Library. *Colorado Chicano Movement History Portal*. Website. Available at HTTP: <chicano.cvlsites.org/> (Accessed 3 January 2018).

Colorado State University-Pueblo. *Colorado Chicano Movement Archives*. Facebook page. Available at HTTP: <www.facebook.com/coloradochicanomovement> (Accessed 3 January 2018).

Colorado State University-Pueblo. *University Archives and Special Collections*. Website. Available at HTTP: <www.csupueblo.edu/library/archives/index.html> (Accessed 3 January 2018).

Cuadraz, Gloria H. "Ethico-Political Dilemmas of a Community Oral History Project: Navigating the Culture of the Corporate University." *Social Justice* 38, no. 3 (2011): 17–32.

Denver Public Library. *Creating Communities*. Online. Available at HTTP: <www.drupal.org/node/903926> (Accessed 3 January 2018).

Digital Preservation Coalition. *The Digital Preservation Handbook*. Online. Available at HTTP: <http://dpconline.org/handbook> (Accessed 3 January 2018).

Digital Public Library of the United States. *Website*. Available at HTTP: <dp.la/> (Accessed 3 January 2018).

Digital Rebellion. *Video Space Calculator*. Online. Available at HTTP: <www.digital rebellion.com/webapps/videocalc> (Accessed 3 January 2018).

East Texas War and Memory Project, Texas A&M University at Commerce. *Website*. Available at HTTP: <sites.tamuc.edu/memory> (Accessed 3 January 2018).

Fernandez, Natalia. "Beyond a Box of Documents: The Collaborative Partnership behind the Oregon Chinese Disinterment Documents Collection." *Journal of Western Archives* 4, no. 1 (2013), Online. Available at HTTP: <digitalcommons.usu.edu/westernarchives/vol4/iss1/5/> (Accessed 3 January 2018).

Fernandez, Natalia. 5 June 2015. Interview with Beverly B. Allen and Fawn-Amber Montoya.

Fernandez, Natalia. "Latinos en Oregon: Sus Voces, Sus Historias, Su Herencia: A Latino Oral History Project." Online. Available at HTTP: <ir.library.oregonstate.edu/xmlui/bitstream/handle/1957/59415/20160624-RBMS-Fern%C3%A1ndezNatalia-Latinos Oreg%C3%B3n.pdf?sequence=2> (Accessed 3 January 2018).

Fernandez, Natalia. "Oregon Chinese Disinterment Documents: Creating an Online Exhibit." Online. Available at HTTP: <ir.library.oregonstate.edu/xmlui/handle/1957/35839> (Accessed 3 January 2018).

Fernandez, Natalia. "The Oregon Multicultural Archives and the Miracle Theatre Group." Online. Available at HTTP: <ir.library.oregonstate.edu/xmlui/handle/1957/40090?show=full> (Accessed 3 January 2018).

Fernandez, Natalia. "The Oregon Multicultural Archives: Assisting Communities Document Their Histories Through Digital Stewardship and Archival Education." Online. Available at HTTP: <studylib.net/doc/13841936/oregon-multicultural-archives-assisting-communities-docum. . .> (Accessed 3 January 2018).

Flinn, Andrew. "Archival Activism: Independent and Community-led Archives, Radical Public History and the Heritage Professions." *InterActions: UCLA Journal of Education and Information Studies* 7:2, article 6. Online. Available at HTTP: <escholarship.org/uc/item/9pt2490x> (Accessed 3 January 2018).

Gavazzi, Stephen M. "Making Use of Assessment Findings in Optimizing Town-Gown Relationships." *Assessment Update*. 28, no. 2 (March/April 2016):1–16.

Gavazzi, Stephen M., Michael Fox, and Jeff Martin. "Understanding Campus and Community Relationships through Marriage and Family Metaphors: A Town-Gown Typology." *Innovative Higher Education* 39, no. 5 (November 2014): 361–374.

Goldsmith, Barbara. "Digitizing Video for Long-Term Preservation: An RFP Guide and Template." 2013. Online. Available at HTTP: <memoriav.ch/wp-content/uploads/2014/07/VARRFP.pdf> (Accessed 3 January 2018).

Gracy III, David B. "Is there a Future in the Use of Archives." *Archivaria* 24 (Summer 1987): 9.

Grateful Dead Archive Online. *Website.* Available at HTTP: <www.gdao.org/help> (Accessed 3 January 2018).

Hawker, Christopher. "The Three Keys to a Successful Crowd Funding Campaign" Online. Available at HTTP: <www.entrepreneur.com/article/234298> (Accessed 3 January 2018).

Heaney, Tom. "The Illusive Ground Between Town and Gown." *New Directions for Adult & Continuing Education* 139 (Fall 2013): 28–37.

Henry, Linda. "Archival Advisory Committees: Why?" *American Archivist* 48, no. 3, (Summer 1985): 316.

Hensen, Pamela M. "Oral History Seminar." Online. Available at HTTP: <www.american.edu/cas/history/public/upload/Oral-History-2005-Henson.pdf> (Accessed 3 January 2018).

Houston Metropolitan Research Center. *Website.* Available at HTTP: <www2.houstonlibrary.org/hmrc/> (Accessed 3 January 2018).

JISC. *Digital Preservation: Continued Access to Authentic Digital Assets.* Briefing paper. 2006: 5. Online. Available at HTTP: <www.webarchive.org.uk/wayback/archive/20140615231719/http://www.jisc.ac.uk/media/documents/publications/digitalpreservationbp.pdf> (Accessed 3 January 2018).

Kaltura. *Website.* Available at HTTP: <https://corp.kaltura.com/> (Accessed 3 January 2018).

Krizack, Joan. 12 June 2015. Interview with Beverly B. Allen and Fawn-Amber Montoya.

Larson, Mary A. "Steering Clear of the Rocks: A Look at the Current State of Oral History Ethics in the Digital Age." *The Oral History Review* 40, no. 1 (2013): 36–49.

Lesbian Herstory Archives. *Mission Statement.* Online. Available at HTTP: <www.lesbianherstoryarchives.org/history.html#mission> (Accessed 3 January 2018).

MacKay, Nancy. *Curating Oral Histories: From Interview to Archive.* "Chapter 5. Ethical Considerations." 2nd ed. (New York: Routledge, 2016).

Martin, Patricia Preciado. *Songs My Mother Sang to Me: An Oral History of Mexican American Women.* (Tucson, AZ: University of Arizona Press, 1992).

Mazé, Elinor A. "Metadata: Best Practices for Oral History Access and Preservation." Online. Available at HTTP: <ohda.matrix.msu.edu/2012/06/metadata/> (Accessed 3 January 2018).

Mecagni, Giordana. 24 November 2015. Phone conversation with Beverly B. Allen.

Montoya, Fawn-Amber. "Salt Creek Memory Project." Online. Available at HTTP: <www.youtube.com/watch?v=04zMYj1AI0k> (Accessed 3 January 2018).

Morini, Ryan. 26 July 2016. Email to Beverly B. Allen.

National Archives. *Appendix A: Tables of File Formats.* Online. Available at HTTP: <www.archives.gov/records-mgmt/policy/transfer-guidance-tables.html#digitalaudio> (Accessed 3 January 2018).

National Coalition for History. *New Federal Rule Exempts Oral History From IRB Review.* Online. Available at HTTP: <historycoalition.org/2017/01/19/new-federal-rule-exempts-oral-history-from-irb-review/> (Accessed 3 January 2018).

Neuenschwander, John. *Oral History as a Teaching Approach*. (Washington DC: National Education Association, 1976).

Northeastern University. *Diversity Enrollment statistics*. 2016. Online. Available at HTTP: <www.northeastern.edu/admissions/wp-content/uploads/2015/08/Diversity_One Pager2015.pdf> (Accessed 3 January 2018).

Northeastern University. *Documenting Boston's Communities*. Online. Available at HTTP: <library.northeastern.edu/archives-special-collections/about/documenting-diversity> (Accessed 3 January 2018).

Northeastern University. *Our Marathon: The Boston Bombing Digital Archives*. Website. Available at HTTP: <www.northeastern.edu/nulab/our-marathon-the-boston-bombing-digital-archive-2/> (Accessed 3 January 2018).

NSDA. *Levels of Digital Preservation*. Online. Available at HTTP: <ndsa.org/activities/levels-of-digital-preservation/> (Accessed 3 January 2018).

OCLC. *ArchiveGrid*. Website. Available at HTTP: <www.oclc.org/research/themes/research-collections/archivegrid> (Accessed 3 January 2018).

Okihiro, Gary Y. "Oral History and the Writing of Ethnic History: A Reconnaissance into Method and Theory." *The Oral History Review* 9 (1981): 27–46.

Oral History Association. *Oral History Defined*. Online. Available at HTTP: <www.oral history.org/about/do-oral-history/> (Accessed 3 January 2018).

Oral History Association. *Principles and Best Practices*. Online. Available at HTTP: <www. oralhistory.org/about/principles-and-practices/> (Accessed 3 January 2018).

Oral History Association. *Website*. Available at HTTP: <www.oralhistory.org/> (Accessed 3 January 2018).

Oral History Online. *Oral History Metadata Synchronizer*. Online. Available at HTTP: <www.oralhistoryonline.org/> (Accessed 3 January 2018).

Oregon State University. *Enrollment statistics, 2016*. Online. Available at HTTP: <oregon state.edu/admin/aa/ir/sites/default/files/enroll-fall-2016.pdf> (Accessed 3 January 2018).

Oregon State University. *Juntos Program*. Online. Available at HTTP: <opencampus.oregon state.edu/programs/juntos/> (Accessed 3 January 2018).

Ortega, José. "Barrio de Salado. Community Unification and Improvement." Online. Available at HTTP: <prezi.com/wnekugcdp13c/salt-creek/> (Accessed 3 January 2018).

Ortiz, Paul. 22 June 2015. Interview with Beverly B. Allen and Fawn-Amber Montoya.

Owen, Trevor. "The Theory and Craft of Digital Preservation." *LIS Scholarship Archive Preprints*. Online. Available at HTTP: <https://osf.io/preprints/lissa/5cpjt/> (Accessed 22 January 2018).

Oxford University Press. *The Oral History Review*. Online. Available at HTTP: <academic.oup.com/ohr> (Accessed 3 January 2018).

Popup Archive. *Website*. Available at HTTP: <www.popuparchive.com/> (Accessed 3 January 2018).

Ritchie, Don. *Doing Oral History*. (New York: Twayne, 1995).

Ritchie, Don. *Doing Oral History*. 3rd edition. (New York: Oxford University Press, 2014).

Schneider, William. *So They Understand: Cultural Issues in Oral History*. (Logan, UT: Utah State University Press, 2002).

Shopes, Linda. "Negotiating Institutional Review Boards." Online. Available at HTTP: <www.historians.org/publications-and-directories/perspectives-on-history/march-2007/institutional-review-boards> (Accessed 3 January 2018).

Shopes, Linda. "Oral History, Human Subjects and Institutional Review Boards." Online. Available at HTTP: <www.oralhistory.org/about/do-oral-history/oral-history-and-irb-review/> (Accessed 3 January 2018).

Skinner, Katherine and Matt Schultz, eds. "A Guide to Distributed Digital Preservation." Online. Available at HTTP: <open.bu.edu/bitstream/handle/2144/1351/GDDP_Educopia.pdf?sequence=1> (Accessed 3 January 2018).

Society of American Archivists. *Donating Your Personal or Family Papers to a Repository.* Online. HTTP: <http://www2.archivists.org/publications/brochures/donating-family recs> (Accessed 3 January 2018).

Society of American Archivists. *SAA Core Values Statement and Code of Ethics.* Online. Available at HTTP: <www2.archivists.org/statements/saa-core-values-statement-and-code-of-ethics> (Accessed 3 January 2018).

Society of American Archivists. *Website.* Online. Available at HTTP: <www2.archivists.org/> (Accessed 3 January 2018).

Sommer, Barbara W. and Mary Kay Quinlan. *The Oral History Manual.* 2nd ed. (Lanham, MD: Altamira Press, 2009).

University of Florida. *Common data set.* 2016–17. Online. Available at HTTP: www.ir.ufl.edu/CDS/Main_cds2016-2017.pdf (Accessed 3 January 2018).

University of Florida. *Mission Statement.* Online. Available at HTTP: <www.registrar.ufl.edu/catalog1011/administration/mission.html> (Accessed 3 January 2018).

University of Florida. Samuel Proctor Oral History Program. *Education and 4+1 BA/MA.* Online. Available at HTTP: <oral.history.ufl.edu/research/education/> (Accessed 3 January 2018).

U.S. Census. *Boston City, Massachusetts Population Estimates.* 1 July 2017. Online. Available at HTTP: <www.census.gov/quickfacts/table/PST045215/2507000> (Accessed 3 January 2018).

U.S. Census. *Commerce City, Texas Population Estimates.* 1 July 2016. Online. Available at HTTP: <www.census.gov/quickfacts/table/PST045216/4816240> (Accessed 3 January 2018).

U.S. Census. *Corvallis City, Oregon Population Estimates.* 1 July 2016. Online. Available at HTTP: <www.census.gov/quickfacts/table/PST045216/4115800,00> (Accessed 3 January 2018).

U.S. Census. *Gainesville City, Florida Population Estimates.* 1 July 2016. Online. Available at HTTP: <www.census.gov/quickfacts/table/PST045216/1225175,4115800,00> (Accessed 3 January 2018).

U.S. Census. *Pueblo City, Colorado Population Estimates.* 1 July 2016. Online. Available at HTTP: <www.census.gov/quickfacts/fact/table/CO/PST045216> (Accessed 3 January 2018).

U.S. Department of Health and Human Services. *Federal Policy for the Protection of Human Subjects.* Online. Available at HTTP: <www.hhs.gov/ohrp/regulations-and-policy/regulations/common-rule> (Accessed 3 January 2018).

Vimeo. *UF Gator Tales.* Online. Available at HTTP: <vimeo.com/119245728> (Accessed 3 January 2018).

Wakimoto, Diana K., Christine Bruce and Helen Partridge. "Archivist as Activist: Lessons from Three Queer Community Archives in California." *Archival Science* 13: 293.

Weddle, Andrea. 15 August 2013. *Commerce Journal* (Commerce, Texas).

Weddle, Andrea. 16 June 2015. Interview with Beverly B. Allen and Fawn-Amber Montoya.

Weddle, Andrea, Hayley Hasik, and Jackson Dailey. "Redefining the Undergraduate: Using Oral History Projects to Promote Undergraduate Scholarship in the Archives." *Archival Outlook* (January/February 2014): 3, 24.

Wurl, Joel. "Ethnicity as Provenance: In Search of Values and Principles for Documenting the Immigrant Experience." *Archival Issues* 29, no.1 (2005): 65–76.

YouTube. *Terms of Service*. Online. Available at HTTP: <www.youtube.com/static?gl= CA&template=terms> (Accessed 3 January 2018).

Yow, Valerie Raleigh. *Recording Oral History: A Practical Guide for Social Scientists*. (Thousand Oaks, CA: Sage Publications, 1994).

Zastrow, Jan. "Crowdsourcing Cultural Heritage: 'Citizen Archivists' for the Future." *Computers in Libraries* 34, no. 8 (Oct 2014): 21–23.

APPENDIX B

Further Reading

Books

Brecher, Jeremy. *History from Below: How to Uncover and Tell the Story of Your Community.* (West Cornwall, CT: Commonwork/Advocate Press, 1995).

Corrado, Edward M. and Heather Moulaison Sandy. *Digital Preservation for Libraries, Archives, and Museums.* (Lanham, MD: Rowman & Littlefield, 2017).

MacKay, Nancy. *Curating Oral Histories: From Interview to Archive.* (Walnut Creek, CA: Left Coast Press, 2016).

MacKay, Nancy, Mary Kay Quinlan, and Barbara W. Sommer. *Community Oral History Toolkit.* (Walnut Creek, CA: Left Coast Press, 2013).

Mercier, Laurie and Madeline Buckendorf. *Using Oral History in Community History Projects.* (Los Angeles, CA: Oral History Association, 2007).

Neuenschwander, John A. *A Guide to Oral History and the Law.* (New York: Oxford University Press, 2014).

Slim, Hugo, Paul Richard Thomson, Olivia Bennett, and others. *Listening for a Change: Oral Testimony and Community Development.* (Philadelphia, PA: New Society Publishers, 1995).

Wood, Linda. *Oral History Projects in your Classroom.* (Carlisle, PA: Oral History Association, 2001).

Articles

Allen, Beverly B., Dana EchoHawk, Rhonda Gonzales, Fawn-Amber Montoya, et al. "Yo Soy Colorado: Three Collaborative Hispanic Cultural Heritage Initiatives." *Collaborative Librarianship,* 4, no. 2 (2012): 2. Online. Available at HTTP: digitalcommons. du.edu/collaborativelibrarianship/vol4/iss2/2/.

Berry, Charlotte and Lucy MacKeith. "Colliding Worlds in the Curatorial Environment: The Archivist and the Activist." *Journal of the Society of Archivists* 28, no. 2 (2007): 139–149.

Calhoun, Diane C., Catherine Jordan, and Saren D. Seifer. "Community-engaged scholarship: Is faculty work in communities a true academic enterprise?" *Academic Medicine* 80, no.4 (2005): 317–21.

Chau, Mary, Jane Nichols, and Elizabeth Nielsen. *Future directions for the Oregon Multicultural Archives*. Online. Available at HTTP: <hdl.handle.net/1957/17109> (Accessed 22 January 2018).

Daniel, Dominique. "Archival Representations of Immigration and Ethnicity in North American History: From the Ethnicization of Archives to the Archivization of Ethnicity." *Archival Science* 14, no. 2 (2014): 69–203.

Fernandez, Natalia M. "Beyond a Box of Documents: The Collaborative Partnership Behind the Oregon Chinese Disinterment Documents Collection." *Journal of Western Archives* 4, no. 1 (2014). Online. Available at HTTP: <http://digitalcommons.usu.edu/westernarchives/vol4/iss1/5/> (Accessed 22 January 2018).

Flinn, Andrew. "Independent Community Archives and Community-generated Content: 'Writing, Saving and Sharing our Histories.'" *Convergence* 16, no. 1 (2010): 39–51.

Gardiner, Gabrielle, Jemima McDonald, Alex Byrne, and Kirsten Thorpe. "Respect, Trust and Engagement: Creating an Australian Indigenous Data Archive." *Collection Building* 30, no. 4 (2011): 148–152.

Grimm, Tracy and Chon Noriega. 2013. "Documenting Regional Latino Arts and Culture: Case Studies for a Collaborative, Community-Oriented Approach." *American Archivist* 76, no. 1 (2013): 95–112.

Haskins, Ekaterina. "Between Archive and Participation: Public Memory in a Digital Age." *Rhetoric Society Quarterly* 37, no. 4 (2007): 401–422.

High, Steven C., Lisa Ndejuru, and Kristen O'Hare. "Sharing Authority: Community-University Collaboration in Oral History, Digital Storytelling, and Engaged Scholarship." *Journal of Canadian Studies* 43, no. 1 (2009): 12–258.

Huvila, Isto. "Participatory Archive: Towards Decentralized Curation, Radical User Orientation, and Broader Contextualization of Records Management. *Archival Science* 8, no. 1 (2008): 15–36.

Ketelaar, Eric. "Archival Temples, Archival Prisons: Modes of Power and Protection." *Archival Science* 2 (2002): 221–238.

Kline, Carrie Nobel. "Giving It Back: Creating Conversations in Interpreting Community Oral History." *The Oral History Review* 23, no. 1 (1996): 19–39.

Krizack, Joan D. "Preserving the History of Diversity: One University's Efforts to Make Boston's History More Inclusive." *RBM: A Journal of Rare Books, Manuscripts, & Cultural Heritage* 8, no. 2 (2007): 125–132.

Lyons, John F. "Integrating the Family and the Community into the History Classroom: An Oral History Project in Joliet, Illinois." *History Teacher* 40, no. 4 (2007): 481–491.

Matusiak, Krystyna K., Allison Tyler, Catherine Newton, and Padma Polepeddi. "Finding access and digital preservation solutions for a digitized oral history project: A case study." *Digital Library Perspectives* 33, no 2 (2017): 88–99.

Neal, Kathryn M. "Cultivating Diversity: The Donor Connection." *Collection Management* 27, no. 2 (2002): 33–42.

Shilton, Katie and Ramesh Srinivasan. "Participatory Appraisal and Arrangement for Multicultural Archival Collections. *Archivaria* 63 (2007): 87–101.

Shopes, Linda. "Oral History and the Study of Communities: Problems, Paradoxes, and Possibilities." *Journal of American History* 89, no. 2 (2002): 588–598.

Somerville, Mary M. and Dana EchoHawk. "Recuerdos Hablados/Memories Spoken: Toward the Co-creation of Digital Knowledge with Community Significance." *Library Trends* 59, no. 4 (2011): 650–662.

Spring, Kathleen and Brenda DeVore Marshall. "Building Bridges with Boats: Preserving Community History through Intra- and Inter-Institutional Collaboration." *Advances in Librarianship* 37 (2013): 3–29.

Vallier, John. "Sound Archiving Close to Home: Why Community Partnerships Matter." *Notes* 67, no. 1 (2010): 39–49.

Web Resources

Farrell, Shanna. "Crowdfunding for Oral History Projects." *OUP Blog*, 2014. Available at HTTP: <blog.oup.com/2014/05/crowdfunding-oral-history-projects> (Accessed 22 January 2018).

McGrath, Jim, Alicia Peaker, Ryan Cordell, Elizabeth Maddock Dillon, et al. "Our Marathon: The Boston Bombing Digital Archive." Online. Available at HTTP: <www.northeastern.edu/marathon. (Accessed 3 January 2018).

Oral History Association. *Oral History in the Digital Age*. Online. Available at HTTP: <ohda.matrix.msu.edu> (Accessed 22 January 2018).

Ortiz, Paul. "Oral History Workshop." 2014. Online. Available at HTTP: </oral.history. ufl.edu/files/2014-Oral-History-Workshop.pdf> (Accessed 22 January 2018).

Samuel Proctor Oral History Program. University of Florida. *Volunteer Information Handbook*. Online. Available at HTTP: <oral.history.ufl.edu/files/Volunteer-Handbook-2014.pdf> (Accessed 22 January 2018).

Southern Oral History Program, University of North Carolina at Chapel Hill. *A Practical Guide to Oral History*. Online. Available at HTTP: <sohp.org/files/2013/11/A-Practical-Guide-to-Oral-History_march2014.pdf> (Accessed 22 January 2018).

Southern Oral History Program, University of North Carolina at Chapel Hill. *Student Interviewer Guidelines*. Online. Available at HTTP: <sohp.org/files/2012/04/Student-Handbook_not-specific-to-a-course.pdf> (Accessed 22 January 2018).

Walsh, David Austin. "How to Get Funding for Oral History." Online. Available at HTTP: <historynewsnetwork.org/article/154366> (Accessed 22 January 2018).

Websites

General

History Matters. *Oral History Online*. Website. Available at HTTP: <historymatters.gmu. edu/mse/oral/online.html> (Accessed 25 January 2018).

Oral History Association. *Website*. Available at HTTP: <www.oralhistory.org> (Accessed 22 January 2018).

Content Management Systems

Drupal. *Website*. Available at HTTP: <www.drupal.org > (Accessed 22 January 2018).

DSpace. *Website*. Available at HTTP: <www.dspace.org> (Accessed 22 January 2018).

E-Discussion Lists

H-OralHist. *Website*. Available at HTTP: <networks.h-net.org/h-oralhist> (Accessed 22 January 2018).

Equipment for Oral History

Vermont Folklife Center. *Digital Audio Recording Equipment Guide*. Online. Available at HTTP: <www.vermontfolklifecenter.org/archive/res_audioequip.htm> (Accessed 22 January 2018).

Grant Funding

Baylor University. *Website*. Available at HTTP: <www.baylor.edu> (Accessed 22 January 2018).

Foundation Center. *Foundation Finder*. Online. Available at HTTP" <foundationcenter. org/findfunders/foundfinder> (Accessed 22 January 2018).

Grants.gov. *Website*. Available at HTTP: <grants.gov> (Accessed 22 January 2018).

Institute of Museum and Library Services. *Website*. Available at HTTP: <www.imls.gov/grants/apply-grant/available-grants> (Accessed 22 January 2018).

National Endowment for the Humanities. *Website*. Available at HTTP: <www.neh.gov/grants> (Accessed 22 January 2018).

National Historical Publications and Records Commission. *Website*. Available at HTTP: <www.archives.gov/nhprc> (Accessed 22 January 2018).

Oral History Association. *Emerging Crisis Research Fund*. *Website*. Available at HTTP: <www.oralhistory.org/award/emerging-crisis-research-fund> (Accessed 22 January 2018).

Storycorps. *Website*. Available at HTTP: <storycorps.org/your-library> (Accessed 22 January 2018).

Institutional Review Boards

Bard. *Website*. Available at HTTP: <inside.bard.edu/irb/interview_oral_hist> (Accessed 22 January 2018).

Oral History Association. *Human Subjects and Institutional Review Boards Bibliography*. Online. Available at HTTP: <www.oralhistory.org/bibliography-human-subjects-and-institutional-review-boards> (Accessed 22 January 2018).

University of Massachusetts. *Human Subjects Research Policy*. Online. Available at HTTP: <www.umass.edu/research/policy/human-subjects-research-policy> (Accessed 22 January 2018).

Metadata Best Practices

Oral History Association. *Metadata: Best Practices for Oral History Access and Preservation*. Online. Available at HTTP: <ohda.matrix.msu.edu/2012/06/metadata> (Accessed 22 January 2018).

Social Media

Groundswell. *Oral History for Social Change Blog*. Available at HTTP: <www.oralhistoryforsocialchange.org/blog> (Accessed 22 January 2018).

University of Florida. *Samuel Proctor Oral History Program*. Facebook Page. Available at HTTP: <www.facebook.com/OralHistoryProgram/?fref=ts> (Accessed 22 January 2018).

University of Florida. *Samuel Proctor Oral History Program Podcasts*. Online. Available at HTTP: <ufdc.ufl.edu/AA00031673/00001/citation> (Accessed 22 January 2018).

Software for Oral History

Audio Recording/Editing Software

Adobe Audition CC. *Website*. Available at HTTP: <www.adobe.com/products/audition> (Accessed 22 January 2018).
Audacity. *Website*. Available at HTTP: <audacityteam.org> (Accessed 22 January 2018).

Transcription Guides

Baylor University. *Transcribing Oral History*. Online. Available at HTTP: <www.baylor.edu/content/services/document.php/66438.pdf> (Accessed 22 January 2018).
Baylor University. *Style Guide: A Quick Reference for Editing Oral Histories*. Online. Available at HTTP: <www.baylor.edu/oralhistory/doc.php/14142.pdf> (Accessed 22 January 2018).

Transcribing Software

Express Scribe. *Website*. Available at HTTP: <express-scribe.en.softonic.com> (Accessed 22 January 2018).
Google Transcribe. *Website*. Available at HTTP: <transcribe.wreally.com> (Accessed 22 January 2018).
InqScribe. *Website*. Available at HTTP: www.inqscribe.com (Accessed 22 January 2018).

Video editing

Adobe Premiere Pro. *Website*. Available at HTTP: <www.adobe.com/products/premiere.html> (Accessed 22 January 2018).
Final Cut Pro. *Website*. Available at HTTP: <www.apple.com/final-cut-pro> (Accessed 22 January 2018).
iMovie. *Website*. Available at HTTP: <www.apple.com/mac/imovie> (Accessed 22 January 2018).

Other software

Oral History Online. *Oral History Metadata Synthesizer*. Website. Available at HTTP: <www.oralhistoryonline.org> (Accessed 22 January 2018).

Streaming Video

Internet Archive. *Website*. Available at HTTP: <archive.org/index.php> (Accessed 22 January 2018).
Kaltura. *Website*. Available at HTTP: <corp.kaltura.com/Products/Video-Applications/Kaltura-Mediaspace-Video-Portal> (Accessed 22 January 2018).

Web Guides to Doing Oral History

Baylor University Institute for Oral History. *Website*. Available at HTTP: www.baylor. edu/oralhistory (Accessed 22 January 2018).

Nebraska State Historical Society. *Capturing the Past: An Online Oral History Primer*. Online. Available at HTTP: <www.nebraskahistory.org/lib-arch/research/audiovis/oral_history/index.html> (Accessed 22 January 2018).

Northeastern University. *Oral History Toolkit*. Online. Available at HTTP: <library.north eastern.edu/sites/default/files/public/atttachments/FIELD_PAGE_FILES/2016/oral_history_toolkit2.pdf> (Accessed 22 January 2018).

Oral History Association. *Web Guides to Doing Oral History*. Online. Available at HTTP: <www.oralhistory.org/web-guides-to-doing-oral-history> (Accessed 22 January 2018).

University of Florida. *Tutorials: Beginning an Oral History Project*. Online. Available at HTTP: <oral.history.ufl.edu/research/tutorials> (Accessed 22 January 2018).

APPENDIX C

Sample Forms, Policies and Outreach Materials

Advisory Board Guidelines

Colorado State University-Pueblo Archives. Colorado Chicano Movement Archives Advocates Mission Statement.

Catalog Records

University of Florida Libraries. *Catalog Records*. Online. Available at HTTP: <ufdc.ufl.edu/oral/results/?t=oral%20history&yr1=1950&yr2=2017> (Accessed 2 February 2, 2018).

University of Florida. Digital Repository. *Amy Crisp Oral History*. Online. Available at HTTP: <ufdc.ufl.edu/AA00031951/00001/citation> (Accessed 2 February 2018).

Finding Aids

Oregon State University. *Oregon Multicultural Archives Oral History Collection*. *Website*. Available at HTTP: <scarc.library.oregonstate.edu/findingaids/?p=collections/finding aid&id=1924> (Accessed 2 February 2018).

University of North Carolina. Southern Oral History Program. *Southern Oral History Program Collection*. Website. Available at HTTP: <finding-aids.lib.unc.edu/04007/#d1e1215> (Accessed 2 February 2018).

University of North Carolina. Southern Oral History. *Oral History Interview with William Culp*. Online. Available at HTTP: <docsouth.unc.edu/sohp/K-0277/menu.html> (Accessed 2 February 2018).

Forms and Policies

Colorado State University-Pueblo. *University Archives and Special Collections Collection Policy*. Online. Available at HTTP: <guides.library.csupueblo.edu/c.php?g=503493&p=3731106> (Accessed 2 February 2018).

Colorado State University-Pueblo. *Oral History Forms*. Online. Available at HTTP: <guides.library.csupueblo.edu/c.php?g=503511&p=3447381> (Accessed 2 February 2018).

Northeastern University. *Oral History Toolkit. Oral History Checklist.*

Ibid. *Oral History Project Form.*

Ibid. Online. Available at HTTP: <library.northeastern.edu/sites/default/files/public/atttachments/FIELD_PAGE_FILES/2016/oral_history_toolkit2.pdf> (Accessed 2 February 2018).

Informed Consent Agreement

Thank you for agreeing to be interviewed for my San Jose State, School of Information oral history class project. I, [*your name*] am conducting an oral history project titled [*name of project*]. Your interview is valuable to my project.

Your signature constitutes acceptance of the following terms:

1. This interview is conducted as a class project for INFO 284, Fall semester 2016. It will only be accessed by the course instructor, except as stated item #6 or in a separate agreement.
2. The student interviewer has explained the process and answered questions to my satisfaction.
3. My participation is voluntary.
4. I may receive a copy of the interview, either as an audio file or transcript by requesting it from the interviewer.
5. I may use portions of this work for my own publication or for personal and scholarly pursuits.
6. The student interviewer may use all or part of the interview in the e-portfolio or other course work towards a degree.

Signature: _____ Date: _____

Name as you wish it to be used (please print): _____

Institution/Affiliation: _____

Location: _____

Telephone number: (_____) _____-_____

Email address: _____

FIGURE C.1 Informed Consent Agreement. Informed consent forms may be tailored to meet the specific needs of your project. This form was used for interviews conducted by a class.

Northeastern University
University Libraries

ORAL HISTORY PROJECT

For Project Lead
From Pre to Post Production

Complete the Oral History Project Form and submit to Debra Mandel, d.mandel@neu.edu. You will be contacted to meet with Debra and Thomas Bary of the DMC Studios Staff.

Before scheduling interviews, discuss project with DMC Staff:
_____Review Oral History Project and discuss other forms and procedures in the OH Toolkit
_____Discuss post production options and output
_____Schedule and attend 60-90 min. orientation session with project interviewers to include:
_____Review of forms and procedures
_____Review of NUSSO scheduling system
_____Tips for Interviewers
_____Tour of Studio with overview of technical set-up
_____1 or 2 mock interviews in the DMC Video Studio

For Interviewers: Scheduling Interviews
_____Book Video Studio using NUSSO at least 2 weeks in advance of interview. Available hours are Mon-Fri, 9am–5pm. Make arrangements with ITS for any equipment needed for off campus use.
_____Fill out Interview Worksheet
_____Obtain backgroun information from narrator and complete Oral History Narrator Background Worksheet
_____Prepare interview topics and sample questions for narrator
_____Email/Mail Narrator the following 2 weeks before interview and attach:
_____Interview Confirmation Letter to include directions to campus and location for meeting
_____Consent and Release Form
_____Sample Interview Questions
_____Provide name of guest(s) to Access Services at Library-Access Services@neu.edu in advance for library entrance access.

Preparing for the Interview:
_____Gather notes from your background information and any discussions you have had
_____Have list of questions
_____Organize structure of interview (such as starting with background information on the subject and their relationship to the topic.

Day of Interview
_____Meet the narrator at the turnstiles 20 minutes before interview start time and accompany to Studio
_____Give completed Interview Worksheet and give to DMC staff videographer. Keep copy for yourself
_____Give signed Consent and Release Form to videographer
_____Thank narrator (interviewee)
_____Verify post production with DMC staff
_____Arrange to deliver copy of interview and release form to narrator

FIGURE C.2 Oral History Project Checklists. Project checklists can keep you on track and ensure that everyone involved stays on the same page.

Northeastern University
University Libraries

ORAL HISTORY PROJECT

For DMC Studios Staff
From Pre to Post Production

Pre-Production Checklist for DMC Studio Staff
_____Discuss project, review forms and information packet with Project Lead
_____Schedule and lead 60–90 min. orientation session with project team/interviewers. Orientation will include:
_____Introductions
_____Review Other Forms:
_____Consent and Release Form
_____Oral History Interview Worksheet
_____Interview Confirmation Letter
_____Oral History Narrator Form
_____Tips for Interviewers
_____Oral History Project Recording Log
_____Demo NUSSO scheduling system
_____Discuss interview process. Review Tips for Interviewers.
_____Ask if the interview intends to include photographs or other records to accompany the oral history. If yes, refer them to Archives to discuss.
_____Give tour of Studio with overview of technical set-up
_____Conduct 1 or 2 mock interviews in the Studio

DMC Videographer/Technical Crew Responsibilities
_____When narrator and interviewer arrive, begin introductions and explain the filming process and cues
_____Turn the lighting board on and light the subject for the video shoot
_____White balance camera
_____Mic up the narrator and interviewer
_____Conduct sound check. Listen to the audio quality for interviewer and narrator through a headset
_____Additional crew monitors audio and video quality in the control room
_____Give signal for interview to begin
_____When filming is done, ask people to wait a few minutes until they hear the all clear
_____Say goodbyes
_____Check footage (P2 cards) in FCPX
_____Ingest the footage into FCPX

DMC Staff Post-Production
_____Capture footage and output a video file onto the drive
_____Wipe the card and return to inventory
_____Scan the Consent and Release form and Interview Worksheet and send to Archives
_____Student/Archives views recording and completes Oral History Project Recording Log

FIGURE C.2 Continued

Northeastern University
University Libraries

ORAL HISTORY PROJECT FORM

Project Lead/Faculty Member: _____

Email: _____ Phone Number: _____

Course Name & Number: _____

Project Due Date: _____

Date Range of Interviews: _____

Number of Students in Class: _____

Assignments are: _____ Individual _____ Group-based Interview

Format: _____ Audio _____ Video

Library staff support needed—instruction:

    _____ Video production workshop

    _____ Audio production workshop

    _____ Interviewing skills workshop

    _____ Archives consult

Requested media output (recommended):

    _____ mpeg 2, wrapped in a quicktime wrapper, in full HD

    _____ Mp3 or AIFF (audio)

Other: _____

Will interviewee like a copy of the interview? _____

Library staff support needed—production:

    Pro videography assistance _____

    Equipment lending _____

Storage/publishing:

Potential candidate for Digital Repository Service (DRS)? _____ If yes, contact archivist

    and DRS Manager. Website/exhibit space needed? _____

Project Lead will keep original,

Need external Hard Drive? _____

For DMC Staff:

Staff Assigned to Project: _____

_____

Equipment Needed: _____

_____

FIGURE C.3 Oral History Project Form. This form, used when collaborating with a class, is useful for tracking library staff assigned to the project.

[Institution Name] Oral History Project
ORAL HISTORY RELEASE FORM

In consideration of the recording and preservation of my oral history narrative by the [Institution Name] Oral History Project, I, the narrator,

_____,

hereby grant to [Institution Name] the rights to use, reproduce, exhibit or make available in any medium (for example, print publications, video, and/or audio recordings, internet, and/or other media formats and platforms) these recordings for any purpose that [Institution Name] and those acting pursuant to its authority, deem appropriate.

Likewise, [Institution Name] hereby agrees to preserve the products of this oral history interview according to accepted professional standards of responsible custody.

Narrator's name: _____

Narrator's Signature: _____

Date: _____

Narrator's address:
_____ (street or p.o. box)

_____
(city)   (state)   (zip code)

Narrator's phone number: (_____)_____-_____

Interviewer's Signature: _____

Date: _____

FIGURE C.4 Oral History Release Form. Having the narrator sign a release form at the beginning of the project not only improves the university's ability to use oral histories, but also ensures that the narrator understands from the outset that they are agreeing to make the interview available not only at the repository, but also possibly on the internet, and in other venues.

Memorandum of Understanding

MacKay, Nancy. *Curating Oral Histories: From Interview to Archive.* (Walnut Creek, CA: Left Coast Press, 2016). Memorandum of Understanding.
Oregon Multicultural Archives. Memorandum of Understanding.

Memorandum of Understanding (MOU)

This letter summarizes the responsibilities of _____(repository) and the _____ (oral history project). In addition to this document, a legal release agreement form signed by each interviewer and interviewee will accompany each oral history.

The _____ oral history project is responsible for these tasks and for the costs incurred:

- Audio or video record interviews in formats and quality determined by repository,
- Transcribe oral history interviews according to style guidelines provided by repository,
- Deliver signed legal release agreement for each interview,
- Deliver transcript and discs in format agreed upon.

The _____ repository is responsible for these tasks and for the costs incurred:

- Advise in selection and training of interviewers,
- Advise in development of project plan,
- Catalog oral histories for local catalog and WorldCat,
- Format, copy, and bind oral history materials.
- Make copies available for use according to repository's access policy.
- Copyright will be (select one)
- Transferred to the repository
- Retained by the oral history project
- Assigned to the public domain

Number of interviews _____

Time frame for delivery _____

REPOSITORY   ORAL HISTORY PROJECT

Name (print) _____   Name (print) _____

Signature _____   Signature _____

Title _____   Title _____

Date _____   Date _____

FIGURE C.5 Memorandum of Understanding (MOU). When working with a community group on an oral history project, it's always good to have a written agreement which spells out the responsibilities of each party to the agreement. This may help avoid problems down the road.

MEMORANDUM OF UNDERSTANDING

AMONG THE Oregon Multicultural Archives at the Oregon State University
Special Collections and Archives Research Center, Corvallis, Oregon
AND [Project Lead]
[Project Name]

The Project: [Project Name]

This MOU concerns the [Project Name], a project spearheaded by [Project Lead, Title], and in consultation with a project advisory board representing the [community/communities].

Project Objectives:

- To conduct oral history interviews, audio and/or video, with members of the [community/communities].
- To gather physical materials from members of the [community/communities] that document their experiences.
- To use the materials gathered to write and publish a book regarding the [community/communities] of [location], during [date range].
- To develop a model or standard of archiving policy and procedures to provide for culturally responsive archival practices with the [community/communities] oral histories and physical materials.
- To archive – preserve, arrange and describe, and make accessible to the public—the information and materials gathered after the publication of the book tentatively scheduled for 2020 (+/–) or thereabouts.
- To curate an exhibit about the project during/after the book's publication.
- To publish articles, participate in presentations, and/or other related scholarly and community research-based endeavors.

FIGURE C.6 Memorandum of Understanding. This is an example of how an MOU may be modified to accommodate a more complicated set of requirements between parties.

Partner Contributions:

The Oregon Multicultural Archives (OMA) at the Oregon State University Special Collections and Archives Research Center, Corvallis, OR agrees to:

Conducting the Oral History Interviews
- Assist with providing access to and reservations for a location for the oral history interviews, and potentially other project related activities to take place, at the [location], or other identified locations as deemed needed by [Project Lead].
- Loan video and audio equipment for the 20xx-20xx academic year, July 20xx-June 20xx, and potentially grant an extension if requested:
- The OMA will provide a camera and tripod, checked out from the OSU Student Multimedia Services Department, as well as a H4n audio recorder, on loan from the OMA. The equipment will be temporarily stored at the [location] during the time the oral history interviews are being conducted.
- The OMA will provide training to [Project Lead] on how to use the video camera and audio recorder as well as how to transfer the files to the OMA to be archived.
- The OMA will check in and out the video camera and tripod at the end of each academic quarter (September and December 20xx and March and June 20xx—final check in June 20xx) to ensure continued use throughout the academic year.

Archiving the Project Materials
- Oral History Interviews
- Gather copies of the signed oral history interview consent forms.
- For the duration of the project, make the oral history interviews accessible online only to [Project Lead] who will then share the interviews with the project interviewees or anyone else she selects.
- Make edits to the oral history interviews as requested by [Project Lead] in consultation with the project interviewees.
- Make the oral history interviews accessible to the public after the book's publication.
- Abide by the decision made by [Project Lead] and the project advisory board regarding what will occur to the interviews if the book publication is cancelled or prolonged.

FIGURE C.6 Continued

- Physical Collection(s)
- Provide consultation to [Project Lead] and the project advisory board. The OMA will provide options for how to archive the physical materials gathered as part of the project once [Project Lead] deems them to be ready to be archived; an option may be for the OMA to acquire the materials gathered as one collection donated by [Project Lead] and community members, and/or individual community members may choose to donate their materials separately.
- Discuss options for a temporary collection site for physical objects to be housed for the primary purposes of access to [Project Lead] for no more than a year.
- Make the physical collection accessible to the public after an exhibit about the project is curated.
- Discuss fundraising options in support of the project with [Project Lead] and the project advisory board.
- In collaboration with [Project Lead], make the project materials available to whichever host institution curates an exhibit about the stories and/or materials gathered.

[Project Name] agrees to:

Conducting the Oral History Interviews
- In collaboration with OMA, participate in training and management of time and location arrangements with the [location] for gathering the oral history interviews, and potentially other project related activities to take place, at the [location].
- Abide by the training, policies and procedures established with OMA regarding the loaned video and audio equipment for the 20xx-20xx academic year, July 20xx-June 20xx. If needed, [Project Lead] will request for an extension to the equipment loan period.
- Sign and collect the OSU Oral History Agreement and Release Form & Deed of Gift forms to reflect that the data and materials will remain in the [Project] Collection unless otherwise specified by the project and that release time periods and other considerations are yet to be determined.

FIGURE C.6 Continued

Archiving the Project Materials
- Oral History Interviews
  - Ensure that all interviewees and [Project Lead] sign the OMA oral history interview consent form stating that their interviews can be archived by the OMA and be made accessible with the tentative restrictions deemed appropriate by [Project Lead] and the project's advisory board, and after [Project Lead]'s book is published.
  - Listen to the interviews prior to sending the files to the OMA and will note of any edits that need to be made. The interviewee(s) will review the interview and will contact [Project Lead] regarding any edits to be made, who will forward that information to the OMA.
  - Provide the necessary metadata for each interview including: the date and location of the interview, interviewee name, and a short biography.
  - Agree that the oral history interviews will be made accessible to the public after the book's publication.
  - Agree that if the book publication is cancelled and/or an extension required and at the end of the project at publication, [Project Lead] and the project's advisory board will make a decision about what will happen to the collection; options include, but are not limited to, closing the files to public access for a specific time period or deleting all the content gathered.
  - Agree that after the materials are made accessible to the public via the Oregon Multicultural Archives, [Project Lead] and all project members will have access to the collections as members of the general public.
- Physical Collection(s)
  - Temporarily store physical materials at a [location] site accessible to [Project Lead] for research purposes for minimally a year and not to exceed time of publication.
  - Agree that the physical collection will be made accessible to the public after an exhibit about the project is curated.
  - Agree that after the materials are made accessible to the public via the Oregon Multicultural Archives, [Project Lead] and all project members will have access to the collections as members of the general public.

FIGURE C.6 Continued

- Discuss fundraising options in support of the project with the OMA.
- Discuss, in collaboration between the project advisory board and the OMA, the project's unique efforts to establish a policy and procedural model to address the cultural sensitivity involved with collections [community/communities] and physical material collected and donated with regards to areas of traditional knowledge, closed access, sensitive materials, cultural property rights, repatriation and so on.

Both parties and the Board representative acknowledge that this is a working document and amendments may be made as need be throughout the course of the project. Amendments must be reviewed and approved by [Project Lead] and only as deemed necessary, with the project's advisory board consultation.

Signature constitutes agreement with conditions above.

_____

[Project Lead]   Date

_____

[Name], Advisory Board Chair   Date

_____

Multicultural Librarian, Oregon Multicultural Archives   Date

FIGURE C.6 Continued

Mission Statement

Dartmouth College. *Oral History Program Mission Statement*. Online. Available at HTTP: www.dartmouth.edu/~library/rauner/archives/oral_history/?mswitch-redir=classic (Accessed 2 February 2018).

Publicity Materials

Colorado State University-Pueblo. *Author Visit, Donor Recognition Event Flier*. Online. Available at HTTP: <guides.library.csupueblo.edu/ld.php?content_id=36940172> (Accessed 2 February 2018).
Colorado State University-Pueblo. *Postcard Invitation, Dia de la Raza Event*. Online. Available at HTTP: <guides.library.csupueblo.edu/ld.php?content_id=32111524> (Accessed 2 February 2018).
Colorado State University-Pueblo. *La Cucaracha Event Flier*. Online. Available at HTTP: <guides.library.csupueblo.edu/ld.php?content_id=36940500> (Accessed 2 February 2018).
University of Florida. Samuel Proctor Oral History Program. *Gator Tales*. Online. Available at HTTP: <oral.history.ufl.edu/2017/01/30/public-screening-of-gator-tales> (Accessed 2 February 2018).
University of Florida. Samuel Proctor Oral History Program. *Oral History Workshop*. Online. Available at HTTP: <oral.history.ufl.edu/event/4127> (Accessed 2 February 2018).

Transcripts

Colorado State University-Pueblo. *Butch Chavez Oral History Transcript Excerpt*.
Smithsonian Institution. Oral History Interview with Dorothea Lange. Online. Available at HTTP: <www.aaa.si.edu/download_pdf_transcript/ajax?record_id=edanmdm-AAADCD_oh_213615> (Accessed 2 February 2018).
University of Florida. Digital Repository. *Amy Crisp Oral History Interview*. Online. Available at HTTP: <ufdc.ufl.edu/AA00031951/00001/pdf?search=oral+%3dhistory> (Accessed 2 February 2018).

Colorado State University-Pueblo. University Archives and Special Collections
Voices of Protest Oral History Collection (EVOP)

Butch Chavez Oral History Memoir
Part 1 of 2

Interviewed by Brandy Gomez October 15, 2010
Colorado State University-Pueblo Administration Building
Pueblo, Colorado

GOMEZ: This is Brandy Gomez. I'm interviewing Butch Chavez on
           October 15, 2010. This interview is taking place in the admin-
           istration building of CSU-Pueblo. The interview is sponsored by
           the CSU-Pueblo University Archives and Special Collections, and
           is part of the Southern Colorado Ethnic Heritage and Diversity
           Archives Project. I want to confirm that Mr. Chavez understands
           that this interview is being recorded, and that this recording will
           be preserved at the CSU-Pueblo University Archives.

CHAVEZ: I understand.

GOMEZ: Thank you for agreeing to be interviewed with us. We look
           forward to hearing all your information. Now, can you please
           state your name for us?

CHAVEZ: I'm Butch Chavez.

GOMEZ: And when and where were you born? CHAVEZ: I was born May 8,
           1946, here in Pueblo [CO]. GOMEZ: And, did you grow up in
           Pueblo also?

CHAVEZ: Yes, born and raised, and got into a lot of trouble.

GOMEZ: And have you just lived in Pueblo all your life?

CHAVEZ: No, no.

GOMEZ: Where else have you lived?

FIGURE C.7 A Two-Page Excerpt From An Interview A CSU-Pueblo Undergraduate
Did With A Latino Vietnam Vet.

CHAVEZ: I've lived in Denver after I got out of the service and Littleton [and] in Aurora.

GOMEZ: What jobs have you had?

CHAVEZ: I worked at Martin Marietta, working on the Titan IIIC missile. I did that for about five to six years. And then, I went into the real estate business, and I've been—was in the real estate business for 38 years, up until just last year.

GOMEZ: And what do you do now for a living?

CHAVEZ: I'm retired.

GOMEZ: Retired.

GOMEZ: Enjoying the nice retired life. We know that you're involved in many veterans' organizations now.

CHAVEZ: Yes, I am.

GOMEZ: Can you tell us a little bit about those organizations?

CHAVEZ: Yes. I am a past Vice President of American Legion Riders. It's a motorcycle organization. It's not a gang. We are just a group of veterans that like to ride motorcycles. We all have the same passion and that's helping veterans. One of the major things we do is – or they do – is raise funds to buy care packages for soldiers overseas, and to have a little extra money to help soldiers out in need and veterans as well. But, lately, it seems like when the soldiers deploy, the families are having problems financially, with utilities and stuff. So, we kind of help out if we can.

GOMEZ: That sounds like a wonderful organization.

CHAVEZ: Yes it is. It is.

GOMEZ: And what were you doing before you entered the service?

FIGURE C.7 Continued

APPENDIX D

Glossary

Academy A place of study or training in a special field, such as a college or university; a society or institution of distinguished scholars, artists, or scientists, that aims to promote and maintain standards in its particular field.

Access Ways of making archival materials available to researchers. The term can mean either access to a physical object, such as a letter or printed text, or to digital items.

Advisory Committee Committee including knowledgeable and credible members in their field of expertise from within and outside the University.

Backup Short-term data recovery solution following loss or corruption.

Barrio Spanish term for neighborhood, usually used by the residents of the community. Can be a derogatory term. As used in this book, it is how the community refers to itself.

Cloud A network-based digital storage solution.

Collection Policy A collection policy defines the kinds of records or other archival materials that an archives plans to preserve and make available for research.

Community A group of people who live in the same area (such as a city, town, or neighborhood) or who have the same interests, religion, race, etc.

Community Archiving Independent grassroots efforts initiated by communities to collect, preserve, and make accessible records documenting their own histories outside of mainstream archival institutions.

Copyright The exclusive legal right of the creator to reproduce, publish, distribute, and sell literary, musical, and artistic works. To see how copyright relates to oral history.

Crowdfunding   The use of social media to collect small amounts of money from a large number of individuals to finance a new venture.

Crowdsourcing   The process of obtaining needed services, ideas, or content by soliciting contributions from a large group of people, and especially from an online community, rather than from traditional employees or suppliers.

Digital Preservation   Digital preservation combines policies, strategies and actions to ensure access to reformatted and born digital content regardless of the challenges of media failure and technological change. The goal of digital preservation is the accurate rendering of authenticated content over time.

Informed Consent   A process by which potential narrators are provided information about the oral history project as well as adequate opportunity to ask questions; also a form or agreement which documents the narrator's voluntary decision to participate.

In-Kind   The provision of goods or services instead of monetary compensation.

Joint Stewardship   The sharing of acquisition, ownership and decision-making processes between an archives and a community.

Legal Release Form   A document that transfers copyright in an interview to a designated owner, and may outline restrictions on use of the interview material. The form is signed by the interviewer and the narrator and by any other people whose voices are heard on the recording.

Lossless Digital Format   Lossless format is uncompressed, resulting in no loss of data from the original file.

Lossy Digital Format   Lossy formats are those where data is compressed, or thrown away, as part of the encoding. The MP3 format is widely used for commercial distribution of music files over the web, because the lossy encoding process results in smaller file sizes.

Metadata   Literally data which describes other data, in this context, an oral history interview. There are several kinds of metadata, such as: information about the interview; information about the digital files itself such as file type, codec, file size, and resolution; metadata may also contain information about copyright, provenance and other administrative matters.

Master   Refers to the original version of a recording or interview.

Narrator (also called interviewee or informant)   The person being interviewed. The narrator is chosen because of his or her knowledge and ability to communicate that information.

Oral History   Oral history is a field of study and a method of gathering, preserving and interpreting the voices and memories of people, communities, and participants in past events. (Oral History Association).

Oral History Interview An interview that records an individual's personal recollections of the past and historical events.

Primary Source First-hand information communicated by a witness or a participant in an event or way of life.

Public History History that is seen, heard, read, and interpreted by a popular audience. It expands on the methods of academic history by emphasizing non-traditional evidence and presentation formats, reframing questions, and in the process creating a distinctive historical practice. Public history is also history that belongs to the public. By emphasizing the public context of scholarship, public history trains historians to transform their research to reach audiences outside the academy. (New York University, Graduate School of Public History http://www.nyu.edu/gsas/dept/history/publichistory/main.htm).

RAID (Redundant Array of Independent Discs) Computerized data storage strategy that involves distributing or mirroring data across multiple disk drives.

Recording Abstract (also called a **tape log**) A list of subjects covered in the interview in the order in which they were discussed, usually done at two- to five-minute intervals and identified with a recording time count. It does not include the questions asked and does not have to be in complete sentences, but should be descriptive enough for a user to find specific information on the recording.

Redundancy In preservation context, refers to the creation of multiple copies of digital assets. Simply making copies is one part of a digital preservation plan.

Social Media Websites and applications that enable users to create and share content or to participate in social networking, c.f. Facebook, Twitter, Tumblr, etc.

Tag Used in blogs, site authors attach keyword descriptions (called tags) to identify images or text within their site as a categories or topic. Web pages and blogs with identical tags can then be linked together allowing users to search for similar or related content. If the tags are made public, online pages that act as a Web-based bookmark service are able to index them. Tags can be created using words, acronyms or numbers.

Town and Gown In a college town, the relations between the residents of the town and the students and faculty associated with the school, who in the past wore academic gowns.

Transcript A word-for-word printed copy of the interview.

Digital Terms Glossary

OHDA Digital Audio and Video Glossary of Terms and Concepts: http://ohda.matrix.msu.edu/gettingstarted/glossary/

INDEX

CPSIA information can be obtained
at www.ICGtesting.com
Printed in the USA
LVHW080240190420
653974LV00004B/40